THE HUMOURS OF DONNYBROOK
Dublin's Famous Fair and its Suppression

Maynooth Studies in Local History

GENERAL EDITOR Raymond Gillespie

One of the features of the practice of Irish history in recent years has been the dramatic growth of interest in local and regional history. This has manifested itself in many ways. There have been a number of monographs dealing with particular national problems from a local perspective. Large collections of essays on local topics, usually based on the county, have been published. At the same time there has been a veritable explosion in the number of local historical journals and pamphlets, many available only at parish level. All of these publications have been important in awakening and fostering interest in the study of the local past but they are not without their problems. On the one hand they have tended to insist on the 'particularity' of places and on the other hand they often generalise from local studies to a national pattern.

This series of Maynooth Studies in Local History, whose origins lie in the St. Patrick's College, Maynooth M.A. course in local history instituted in 1992, presents local historical research which attempts another approach. The essays portray not 'particular places' but the experience of different groups of people or of individuals in the past. They explore the evolution of urban and rural communities in Ireland: how they organised themselves for day-to-day life and how they responded to pressures from within the community and to demands for change from regional or national forces.

It is intended to publish a number of studies every year which will focus on these problems from different chronological and geographical perspectives. Such studies will build up a picture of the varying communities of Ireland from the middle ages to the present day and in doing so present local history as the vibrant and challenging discipline that it is.

Maynooth Studies in Local History: Number 4

The Humours of Donnybrook
Dublin's Famous Fair and its Suppression

Séamas Ó Maitiú

IRISH ACADEMIC PRESS

Set in 10 on 12 point Bembo
and published by
IRISH ACADEMIC PRESS LTD
Kill Lane, Blackrock, Co. Dublin, Ireland
and in North America by
IRISH ACADEMIC PRESS LTD
c/o ISBS, 5804 NE Hassalo Street, Portland, OR 97213.

A catalogue record for this title
is available from the British Library.

ISBN 0-7165-2569-0

Printed in Ireland
by ßetaprint Ltd, Dublin.

Contents

ILLUSTRATIONS

Preface

I would like to thank Ray Gillespie, Colm Lennon, Fergus D'Arcy, Danny Parkinson and my wife, Gráinne for their help, and encouragement. I am also grateful to the National Gallery of Ireland for permission to reproduce figure 3.

Introduction and Historical Background

In 1829 a carman named Foley was charged with 'furious driving' in Sackville St. while going to post a letter for a gentleman in the General Post Office. When asked what he had to say for himself he pleaded with the magistrate 'Oh, sir, these is Donnybrook times, and every one is merry now; if you let me off I'll be *aisy* for a week'. The magistrate was not impressed for he fined him £1.[1]

The Dublin carman was expressing a feeling shared by many of the ordinary people throughout Europe for many centuries that their festival time was special, a time set apart from their ordinary lives when the normal rules of behaviour and constraints did not apply. The reaction of the magistrate epitomised the growing attitude of non-participation by the agents of official culture in such popular customs as Donnybrook Fair.[2]

In southern Europe carnival was the greatest popular festival of the year. It was a time of liberation when one could escape the drudgery of everyday life and engage in behaviour which would not be permitted at other times with impunity. Carnival in southern Europe centred on Shrove Tuesday, of course, but Peter Burke has shown that elements of the festival – the 'carnivalesque' – could be found in popular customs in other places and at other times of the year.[3] I would like to investigate in the following pages to what extent Donnybrook Fair was the carnival of Dublin, or to what extent elements of the carnivalesque can be seen in the celebration of the fair.

Burke calls the success of the elite in curtailing, and in many cases, suppressing expressions of popular culture 'the triumph of Lent'.[4] I would like also to look at the objections of officialdom and the agents of official culture in Dublin to the fair, from the mid-seventeenth century to its enforced demise more than a century later.

The historian has a difficulty with popular culture in that it was largely oral. Much of it took the form of festivals such as Donnybrook Fair which were ephemeral by nature. The only records that these popular festivals left behind tend to be by literate outsiders, many of them hostile, such as are found in official documents, police reports and, to a varying degree, newspapers. Even narrative historians might not be disinterested; Beaver Blacker, quoted below, who chronicled the early fair, was a member of the committee formed in 1854 to abolish it.[5]

How is one then to attempt to grasp the mentality of the great bulk of ordinary fair-goers who were the abiding mainstay of the fair? Songs are one source where it may be possible to hear the voice of the man or woman on the Fair Green. But many of these have been mediated to us through brokers or in some cases composed by literate drawing-room entertainers celebrating the popular, and for that reason they may be untrustworthy. By a cautious approach to sources such as songs, prints and especially newspaper reports one can get perhaps indirectly an idea of popular feeling about the fair. While the newspapers no doubt pandered to the feelings of their elite readers their attitude to the fair while largely hostile was at times ambiguous. They also delighted in colour pieces presenting to their readers in the comfort of their armchairs the atmosphere of the Fair Green and the exploits of the lower orders at play. Much of this has the ring of truth about it and gives us an insight into the fun of the fair.

The attitude of the ordinary fair-goer can be further divined in the response of defendants in court cases, such as that of Foley above, and from pieces in satirical magazines and even stallholders' signs, many of which have been recorded.

In the twelfth and thirteenth centuries the Normans stimulated trade in the areas under their control by the establishment of great fairs. The European fair came to England with the establishment of Bartholomew fair in 1133 and Stourbridge chartered by King John in 1211.[6] Bartholomew Fair, being the great fair of London, was often compared to its Dublin counterpart at Donnybrook; both were held at the same time of year and both suppressed in the same year.[7]

In 1204 King John commanded Meiler Fitzhenry, justiciar of Ireland, to build a castle at Dublin and establish a fair at Donnybrook and at three other places in the country. The relevant section of the charter witnessed at Geydinton on 31 August of that year runs as follows:

> We will, also, that there be a fair at Donnyburn [Donnybrook] annually to continue for eight days on the feast of the Invention of the Holy Cross; and another at the Bridge of St. John the Baptist, likewise for eight days, allowing them the like stallages and tolls; and another at Waterford on the Feast of St. Peter in Chains; another at Limerick, on the feast of St. Martin, for eight days, and we command that you cause it to be thus done, and proclamation made, that all merchants should come thither willingly.[8]

John would have been prompted as to where his citizens in Dublin would like to have a fair patented – it is interesting to speculate as to why Donnybrook was chosen. Was it possible that there was a popular gathering already taking place there?

Many of the English fairs which were granted patents by the English sovereigns in the twelfth and thirteenth centuries had already existed from time out of mind and reconstituted by the charter to conform with the flourishing fairs being held on the continent, especially France, to extract revenue from tolls for the local lord.[9]

Two facts about the site would suggest that it was a suitable place where an early gathering may have taken place; it was a border area and an early church site. In communities which were often at war with one another neutral ground on the fringes of the tribal lands was important for parley and inter-tribal barter. Occasional gatherings in the form of fairs would have easily grown up in this way, and from an early date the occasion was used to proclaim laws, with the peace of the fair to allow trade to take place being sacrosanct.[10] In early Ireland the tribal oenach, where exchange took place was held at the borders of territories, which was regarded as neutral ground.[11]

Donnybrook on the banks of the Dodder was on the fringes of the jurisdiction of the city as granted to Dublin by John in 1172.[12] It was situated at a point where there was more than likely a ford over the river where an important road south crossed it. As such it was a meeting place where people from the agricultural hinterland could trade with the city people.

The Fair Green adjoined the ancient graveyard of Donnybrook and fairs and popular gatherings have for long been associated with burial places. This custom appears to go back to pagan times as many fairs are also found near prehistoric burial earthworks, as a survival of a vanished community to which the gathering had probably been vital to the supply of such things as salt, millstones or implements.[13]

The name Donnybrook is a corruption of the Irish Domhnach Broc – the church of Broc. According to Aengus the Culdee, the chronicler from the monastery of Tallaght, Broc was one of the seven daughters of Dallbronach of the Desii of Bregia, and she founded a convent here on the banks of the Dodder around the year 700 dedicated to the Mother of God on what is now the site of the old graveyard in the village of Donnybrook.[14] The name of Domhnach Broc is recorded in *The Martyrology of Donegal*, which under the date 30 September, records the name of Mobi, nun of Domhnach Broc.[15]

Monasteries with their large population, many of who were people seeking refuge and not under monastic rule, developed an important economic function. The first reference to a monastic oenach in the Annals of Ulster is for the year 800 which records the death of a local king in a fall from a horse at the Fair of Mac Cuillin at Lusk in county Dublin.[16]

That trade was carried on at Irish monasteries and holy places from an early time is well attested.[17] Many of the monasteries such as Glendalough have market crosses. From the start of the spread of Christianity an attempt was made to accommodate the popular pagan customs of the day. The old

mid-winter festival became Christmas and the mid-summer celebration became St. John's Eve.[18]

This practice was explicitly enjoined by Pope Gregory the Great on
Bishop Mellitus, working in England in 601, when he advised him not to
destroy the temples of the idols but to convert them into churches and to
substitute their oxen sacrifice with something appropriate.[19] The fact that
Donnybrook Fair was for most of its existence held in August has led to
speculation that it may have its origins in the Festival of Lughnasa, an ancient Celtic celebration held in many parts of Ireland at the beginning of the
month. The evidence just quoted which shows that the original fair was
held much earlier in the year would seem to invalidate such conjecture.[20]

Many of the great ancient assemblies, such as that at Tara, Tailteann, or
Emhain Macha, probably had their origins in funeral games which were
held in honour of the great personages buried at these sites. Two excerpts
from a poem in the Metrical Dinnshenchas describing Aonach Carman
show that as well as observing the ancient ritual much business was conducted at these great fairs and entertainment was provided:[21]

> Three busy markets in the land
> The market of food, the market of livestock,
> The great market of the Greek Foreigners,
> Where were gold and fine raiment.

The description of the different sections of that great assembly are reminis-
cent of the way the later Fair Green of Donnybrook was divided up, each
part with its allotted business carried on there.

Fairs and gatherings such as that at Donnybrook spring more quickly to
mind on hearing the following description, also from the Dinnshenchas, of
that section of the throng at Carman who were less taken up with official
business – indeed these lines echo almost word for word numerous verses
composed in the eighteenth and nineteenth centuries on Donnybrook Fair:

> Pipes, fiddles, gleemen,
> Bone-players and bagpipers;
> A crowd hideous, noisy, profane,
> Shriekers and shouters.

The fair at St. John's Bridge alluded to in the letter of King John was
probably that which was held at St. John's Well near Kilmainham and continued in the form of a mid-summer's festival until it was suppressed in May
of 1834 for similar reasons to that of Donnybrook.[22]

The feast of the Invention of the Holy Cross fell on 3 May. The right of
the citizens to hold the fair was further recognised in two other letters of the

same king, enrolled in the close roll of the sixteenth and seventeenth years of his reign (1214 and 1215) and by the latter the time of holding the fair was extended to fifteen days, with the first two days' revenue given to the archbishop of Dublin.[23]

By charter dated 1241 Henry III confirmed to his citizens of Dublin and their heirs forever the privilege of holding a fair as granted by King John, his father, for fifteen days but changed the time of holding it. Instead of it commencing on the feast of the Invention of the Holy Cross it would now commence on the vigil of the Translation of St. Thomas the Martyr, 3 July, and continue for fifteen days. The archbishop of Dublin would continue to have 'all liberties and free customs' for the first two days of the fair – that is those of the vigil and feast day – the customs and liberties for the remaining thirteen days would belong to the city.[24]

Two subsequent charters further delayed the holding of the fair until later in the year. The first granted in 1280 by Edward I was said to have been granted at the instance of the citizens of Dublin themselves for their greater convenience and changed the date of the commencement of the fair to the eve of the Translation of St. Benedict the Abbot on 11 July.[25]

The second, whose date is uncertain, further postponed the commencement of the fair to the 26 August, which became the traditional date for holding the fair up to its demise. 'From time immemorial' was the usual term used in later years when referring to this date as the official fair day.[26]

Concerning the area in which the fair was held it is recorded that Richard (Strongbow), earl of Pembroke, gave Donnybrook with other lands to Walter de Riddlesford, baron of Bray, in 1173.[27] Being for a time at the beginning of the fourteenth century in the possession of the Baggots of Baggotsrath, Donnybrook passed into the hands of the Fitzwilliam family when they were seised of a carucate of land there.[28] Richard Fitzwilliam was living at Donnybrook in 1524 when his sister married Christopher Ussher and Donnybrook was given to her in a marriage settlement. So began the long association of the Ussher family with the area.[29] The Ussher family built a large mansion in Elizabethan style, long since demolished, which became known as Donnybrook Castle. This family became the first private holders of the patent to Donnybrook Fair when the corporation of Dublin, possibly as the result of a temporary shortage of cash decided to dispose of its right to hold the fair, and it was bought by them sometime in the 1690s.[30]

An entry in the assembly rolls of Dublin of 23 February 1698 records what is probably the transaction in question. On that day the city council, to enable it to raise a sum of £1,250 to pay a debt, ordered a bond under the city seal, and a mortgage for the same on the revenues of, amongst other properties named, certain lands in Donnybrook set to Sir William Ussher.[31] Both possession of the Fair Green and the patent to hold the fair were in the hands of the Ussher family from about this time. What the debt was is not known.

In 1748 the ownership of the Fair Green, but not the patent for holding the fair, passed from the possession of the Ussher family. In that year a Henry Ussher granted several denominations of land, including the Green, to a Catherine Downes, mother of the first Lord Downes, in fee, excepting and reserving unto the said Henry Ussher, as the legal language put it, his heirs and assigns, the benefit and profit of holding the yearly fair in the usual place.[32]

On the death on Henry Ussher in 1756, the right of holding the fair became vested in Sir William Wolseley baronet, his heir-at-law. In 1778, Wolseley, who was described as residing in the city of London, made a lease of the patent to Joseph Madden.[33] This is the first mention of the Madden family, who were to come into possession of the Fair Green and the ownership of the right to hold the fair and were its staunch defenders until the time of its suppression.

Joseph Madden was born in Kilternan, county Dublin around 1742 and had settled in Donnybrook.[34] Joseph died in 1799 and his son came into full possession of the patent in 1812 when by an indenture made in that year between Sir William and John Madden, the son, for the sum of £750, disposed absolutely of his right to the tolls and customs of Donnybrook Fair.[35]

In 1818 these tolls ranged from two pence for every pig, sheep or calf sold to six pence for every horse, mare, mule or ass.[36] These could amount to a considerable sum; in 1817 the amount received in the toll house on Donnybrook Road during Fair Week came to £160, an amount described at the time as 'almost incredible.'[37]

Despite this however it appears that the trading side of the fair was in decline for some time. As early as the 1690s our first eye-witness report of the fair, that of John Dunton, an English bookseller visiting Ireland, was stating that many of the Dublin cattle dealers were venturing further afield than Donnybrook for their purchases. They were travelling to fairs at Banagher and Mullingar for black cattle, sheep, wool and tallow.[38]

A great deal of business was still carried on however, but it came more and more to rely on the horse trade. Being so near a large city with its constant demand for large numbers of draught animals Donnybrook came to rival Ballinasloe as a horse fair. In 1841 the Maddens made a 'scientific calculation' of the numbers of animals passing through the customs' gap which gives us some indication of the number of head involved. Two thousand five hundred horses were brought to the fair for sale, most adapted for the saddle or draught of the lighter kind and 26 were bought by the army.[39]

It is as a pleasure fair however that Donnybrook came to be regarded by the city folk as the nineteenth century wore on and it is in that light that its function of carnival can be seen.

The World of Carnival

The great area of carnival in Europe lay in the southern Catholic countries. But many aspects of carnival, the carnivalesque, were found at other times of the year and in a more widespread area. Examples were the Festival of Fools (28 December) in France and May Day and St. John's Eve in England and other places. In northern Europe the weather more than likely discouraged the holding of carnival at Shrovetide and it was given over to more domestic indoor rituals. May Day and St. John's Eve compensated for it.[1]

To an even greater extent the carnival indulgence in eating and drinking was deferred in the colder north to autumn. Such indulgence was the main attraction at harvest festivals in England and elsewhere. Another widespread occasion for eating and drinking to excess was the Feast of St. Bartholomew on 25 August. Appropriately St. Bartholomew was the patron saint of butchers and in Italy his feast was celebrated by parading a pig through the streets which was later killed, roasted and distributed.[2]

In London Bartholomew Fair, the renowned 'Old Bartlemey', was held annually on his feast day at Smithfield, the centre of the meat trade. The fair day of Donnybrook, 'from time immemorial' was the following day, 26 August. It is not possible to pinpoint exactly when this day came to be regarded as the fair day. Perhaps, like so much else in Dublin, it was done in imitation of the London precedent, but maybe there was some deeper feeling of celebrating the end of summer and the harvest.

St. Bartholomew was also one of the patron saints of shepherds. His feast day was regarded by them as the day on which the sheep were moved from summer to winter quarters, and an occasion of celebration, when they converged on the towns to indulge in eating and drinking.[3] In this regard it should be remembered that Donnybrook was one of the gateways to the Dublin and Wicklow mountains, great sheep-keeping areas.

Fairs, festivals and feast days tended to take place at times when there was light demand for labour. Autumn was a very popular time. E.P. Thompson quotes a survey of the feast day of 132 villages and towns in Oxfordshire about 1730. All of them fell between May and September, with more than three-fifths being in August and September.[4] August, June and October were the most popular months for Irish fairs.

Festivals such as feast days, fairs and wakes were immensely important in the lives of the people. Such was the feeling of festivity and release associ-

Figure 1 Donnybrook Fair (*Dublin Penny Journal*, 16 Nov. 1833)

ated with such occasions that the ordinary people lived their lives 'in re-
membrance of one festival and in expectation of the next'.[5]
The elements of the carnivalesque found in association with popular festivals are indulgence in food and drink, athletic competition such as foot
races, a greater sense of communal solidarity celebrated by music and song,
the playing of pranks and the staging of plays especially those denoting the
inversion of the real world –the world turned upside down. It also included
enhanced sexuality and indulgence in violence.[6]

I would like to examine eye-witness reports of Donnybrook Fair in the
early nineteenth century to see to what extent these motifs were to be found
among the pleasure-seekers on the Fair Green. Festival time was regarded as
a time set apart from the everyday and people showed this symbolically by
donning their good clothes on such occasions. In one of the most famous
songs about the fair, composed by Edward Lysaght, the fair-goer attending
Donnybrook was turned out in the highest fashion of the day. He had:

> His clothes spick and span new, without e'er a speck
> A neat Barcelona tied round his neat neck.[7]

In one of the songs entitled 'The Humours of Donnybrook' the young man speaking of his 'mott', Nosey Nelly McCann, whom he takes to the fair, says of her

> Tis needless to say she was togged in the best,
> She'd a slap-up new suit off the Poddle was dressed
> She'd a grin on her phiz like a hungry bear
> And that was the duckey I streeled to the Fair.[8]

Eating and drinking were pivotal activities on the Fair Green of Donnybrook. If the visitor somehow failed to see the numerous signs strung over the tents catering for the hungry and thirsty, his nose was filled by the odour from the boiling pots around which were gathered numerous groups being fed for a small fee. In one tent in 1823 one eye-witness observed sirloins, ribs, rounds, flanks, shins briskets, six dozen boiled chickens, twenty eight Wicklow hams, kishes of potatoes, carts of bread and gallons of punch.[9]

In order to provide hospitality for the fair-goers leading vintners and hoteliers from the city set up tents on the Fair Green, some of them quite sumptuous. In 1833 a M'Namara of Kevin St. had a tent called 'The Shamrock, Rose and Thistle', and the proprietor of the Carlingford Beefsteak Tavern, Aston Quay had a tent in partnership with another man where the 'grub and lush' were said to be excellent.[10]

In 1820 Thomas Lee of the Shamrock Tavern, Fownes St., erected the 'Shamrock Booth' in 1820 where parties from 'two to a hundred may be certain of being comfortably accommodated on the instant with the best wines, the best spirits, porter, ale cider etc.'.[11] One gourmet was moved to verse:

> Beef, mutton, lamb and veal,
> Donnybrook Fair,
> Wine, cider, porter, ale,
> Donnybrook Fair.
> Whiskey, both choice and pure,
> Man and maids most demure
> Dancing on the ground flure,
> Donnybrook Fair.[12]

Figure 1 features prominently a woman cutting up a large joint of meat called a 'spoleen' and the typical boiling pot found simmering all over the Fair Green can be seen in figure 2, although what is being extracted from it does not look too appetizing.

Those who found the cost of dining out of their reach were not overlooked. Side-stalls with mountains of gingerbread, fruit and cheese were to

Figure 2 'Donnybrook Fair in the Year 1830. Taken on
the spot by George Du Noyer 1830 Registered'

be found all over the Green. The indulgence did not end with the adults. A
great selection of sweets watered the mouths of the children in 1815: 'Mrs.
Clarke's pincushions, Jacob's sugar-sticks, the sweets of Venus, the kisses of
love, black and white lollypaps [*sic*], spice cakes, plaister of Paris comfits,
peppermint tablets, hearts of delight and a thousand others'.[13]

The signs hung over the various establishments advertising the hospitality within are interesting in that they give us some insight into the attitudes
of the ordinary fair-goer. As they were installed to entice people to buy they
would have been designed to mirror the feelings of the customers on the
Fair Green.

In the so-called 'Dame Street' and the other major thoroughfares boards
painted in magnificent colours and flags were to be seen, but these were
reduced to tawdry rags and bric-a-brac in the alleys and by-ways of the
tented town. Some were just amusing and celebrated the 'humours' of the
occasion. Frank Thorpe Porter, the police magistrate, saw two such:

> Here Paddy comes to have a swig,
> A better one he never took;
> And now he'll dance an Irish jig
> With Dolly Dunne of Donnybrook.

The other represented a beehive displaying the following invitation:

> In this hive we're all alive,
> Good whiskey makes us funny:
> So don't pass by but stop and try
> The sweetness of our honey.[14]

The following couplet could be seen in 1822:

> Entertainment for all who pass,
> For horse, or mare, or colt – or ass.[15]

Some of the signs took up national themes. The 'Shamrock, Rose and Thistle' already alluded to, showed two hands united and the slogan:

> Let all do this, and soon you'll see
> *Ould* Ireland as she ought to be.

Other signs celebrated popular heroes of the day. In 1823 a bust of '*Sir* Dan Donnelly' was displayed under which was to be read:

> May friendship abide in each Irish heart,
> May envy and malice away from thee part,
> May the true sons of Ireland never be beat,
> May Halton his antagonists always defeat.[16]

Halton was the current Irish pugilistic champion. In 1833 George Falkner from Kevin St. had a sign depicting Daniel O'Connell, M.P. together with the slogan:

> Oh, my brave Daniel O'Connell!
> Oh, my brave Daniel O'Connell!
> We'll soon see the day,
> And I hope that we may,
> When we'll have the RAW-PEEL of the ONION![17]

The signs could at times be pointedly political. In 1821 the owner of one of the booths displayed a sign showing the funeral of Queen Caroline, the estranged wife of George IV, which had taken place a short time before. There had been trouble at the funeral over the attempt by the authorities to prevent the cortege from going through the centre of London and the populace had attacked the military. The soldiers were depicted on the sign fleeing in terror. The sign was taken down by the police and the press expressed a wish that the spirit licence of the owner of the booth would not be regranted.[18] In the 1840s the signs usually proclaimed that the proprietor was a repealer.

In the less fashionable sections of the fair sundry emblems were displayed. The most common was a simple cross on a hoop. Others included kegs, dirty Bachuses, cracked imperial crowns (no bad caution to visitors, it was remarked), bunches of turnips, barrels and bottles.[19] Real food like a ham were often displayed but the most revolting sign recorded was a dead and half-putrid cat, seen by Prince Pückler-Muskau on his visit to the fair in 1828.[20] At night, many of the signs were illuminated by placing a light behind them.

Some tents simply had their names and addresses on display hoping to attract in patrons from their area of town. Country areas were represented sometimes also. In 1823 one sign read 'The King's County, a-vick!'[21] A tavern-keeper called Lundy from the Strawberry Beds had a tent which attracted all the pretty girls from Chapelizod and Knockmaroon Hill.[22]

In the early 1830s a number of humorous and satirical magazines began to appear in Dublin and quickly built up large circulations.[23] They specialised in reporting the goings-on of people at the theatre, sporting occasions and gatherings of all sorts. The earliest was *Paddy Kelly's Budget* which was started by a Dublin journalist, Alfred Howard, in 1832. Rivals quickly followed; *The Salmagundi, The True Salmagundi* (rivals themselves obviously) and finally *The Penny Satirist* in 1836. The magazines became by-words for fun, and as fair time came round publicans saw the value of using their names to attract crowds looking for 'divarsion' at Donnybrook.

A tent under the name of 'Paddy Kelly's Budget' was an annual feature for many years.[24] In August, 1834 the *True Salmagundi* announced that a pavillion under that name would open at the forthcoming fair. They had licensed George Meade of Hawkin's Street to use their name in the face of stiff competition from other city publicans and hoteliers for the lucrative franchise.[25]

Having sated one's appetite in one of these sumptuous establishments or from a humble boiling pot, competitions such as footraces, horse-races or football matches, another recurrent element of carnival, drew one's attention. The Roman Carnival had races for young and old men, and football matches were common on Shrove Tuesday in England.[26] Down to the early years of the nineteenth century such participatory sports which the Dublin newspapers called 'rural pastimes' seem to have been the main form of entertainment at Donnybrook. The above-mentioned song 'The Humours of Donnybrook' outlines some of them:

> O you lads that are witty from famed Dublin city,
> And you that in pastimes take any delight,

To Donnybrook fly for the time's drying nigh
When fat pigs are hunted and lean cobblers fight;
When maidens so swift run for a new shift;
Men muffled in sacks for a shirt they race there;
There jockeys well booted, and horses sure-footed,
All keep up the Humours of Donnybrook Fair.[27]

These seemingly wholesome frolics were not as innocent as they appear at
first glance. The maidens often ran for the prizes in their underwear and the
young men often wore even less. The victor of a smock race which took
place at Finglas on May Day prepared for the contest

Stript to the waist how bright did she appear
No covering hid her feet, her bosom bare,
And to the wind she gave her flowing hair.[28]

At Donnybrook in 1818 thousands took part in the fun: 'journeymen of all
trades, apprentices, soldiers, sailors, old collegemen, Jews, pickpockets, common council men, carmen, coachmen, constables, giggling spinsters, im-
prudent mothers, servant-maids, demireps, gadding old women and
half-bucks.' The frolicsome games they took part in included 'Kiss in the
ring', 'Thread my needle, Nan' and 'Hunt the slipper'. In the course of
these games the prurient correspondent reported 'a good deal of picturesque
bye-play took place'.[29] These games were also commonly played at wakes.
'Kiss in the ring' had a number of variants, in one of which a man sat on a
chair surrounded by a circle of dancing girls and picked out one of them
who had to kiss him.[30]

Donnybrook was, as we have seen, a source of horses for the Dublin
haulage and car trade. One gets the impression, however, that there was a
large element of competition and showmanship connected with the horse
trading also.

Visitors and newspapers alike make constant reference to the rivalry of
the carmen on the road to and from the fair each year. It was as if the fun of
the fair started in the St. Stephen's Green area of the city where the various
cars for the fair had their stands. The whole area resounded to the cries of
'Any more for de Brook?' as jaunting cars with almost twice their compli-
ment of six passengers were still being loaded up. So keen was the competition among the carmen to engage a fare that the first broken heads, for
which Donnybrook was notorious, were often sported at Stephen's Green.

A motley cavalcade of vehicles was pressed into service for the occasion,
including landaus, jingles, curricles and noddies and although the Sunday
preceding Fair Week was called 'Walking Sunday' to actually have to walk
to the Fair Green was considered a great indignity. In 1815 'two charioteer'

agreed for a wager of a naggin of Costigan's best Sweet Pea (a favourite brand of whiskey) to race to Donnybrook; they overturned and their passengers were thrown onto the road.[31]

Such bravado concerning horses is also alluded to by Jonah Barrington. The purchase of a horse is a notoriously risky business and it was prudent for the prospective buyer to try out his animal before any money changed hands. Consequently there was much dangerous jockeying on the Green and there was a large ditch with a drain and a piece of a wall which the sellers were called upon to 'leather their horses over' before anyone would bid for them. The tumbles the jockeys received were, according to Barrington, 'truly entertaining', although they were often downright dangerous and on occasion lead to deaths.[32]

A third recurrent element in carnival was the performance of a show or play. There was a sense in which the Fair Green became a set on which the fair-goers themselves became actors. The city itself was recreated on this stage and the numerous passages between the tents were given the names of the major thoroughfares of the city such as 'Dame Street', 'Sackville Street' or 'Merrion Square'.[33]

It is not known if there were native indigenous dramas performed at the fair before the commercialisation of leisure. But with the establishment of the circus, the travelling shows and the penny theatres, a new era of entertainment dawned at Donnybrook.

A group of English visitors to Donnybrook in 1811, sitting in tents, 'cogitating and chewing the cud behind the longest pipes this here country affords', contrasted the scene with Bartholomew, Beau, Peckam and other English fairs. They observed that Donnybrook was entirely destitute of amusements – no theatrical amusements, jugglers, wild beasts or birds, no boxing, bustling or even picking of pockets.[34] They agreed among themselves that the Irish were far behind them in sense and civilisation. The newspaper correspondent who overheard them added snidely that this amounted to the English paying others to amuse them while the Irish amused themselves.

Barrington in his celebrated description of the fair in the last decade of the eighteenth century confirms that boxing was a late arrival. He remarked that 'that brutal species of combat, boxing, was never practised at our fairs; and that savage nest and hot-bed of ruffians called the 'Ring', so shamefully tolerated in England, was unknown among the Emeralders'.[35] It did not take long for all that to change, especially when English showmen found out that there was good profit in bringing 'civilisation' to the Irish, their propensity for amusement being as great, if not greater, than was the case at home. The huge crowds which attended Donnybrook must have been the great attraction.

The very next year after the visit of our condescending Englishmen, 1812, an English company made a disastrous start to visiting Ireland. The company, from a London theatre, laid out an equestrian circus in sumptuous style on the Fair Green. Everything was there – except the horses. They failed to arrive. The riders were standing there like pipes without tobacco or tumblers without punch, as the Irish quipped. The *Freeman's Journal* went on to observe that perhaps the English thought it enough to announce the exhibition, build a theatre, and that the Irish, famous for their fertile imagination, would conjure up the rest in their minds![36]

In 1819 equestrian shows and menageries, mostly from England, were a feature of the fair. Upon entering the Green early in the week that year Kent and Cunningham's Booth of Equestrian Excercise first presented itself; then Cooke's Equestrian Troop and Simon's Performing Dogs. Then one met Bannister and Peter's Equestrian Booth, Polito's Menagerie and a booth, not quite finished, of Leech's for wire dancing, comic singing and other amusements. This led on to Germondi's Wonderful Dogs and a separate booth for Polito's elephant. The whole display was said to have surpassed anything yet witnessed in Ireland.[37] From the 1820s on Wombwell's Menagerie was one of the most frequent of all the English shows to visit Donnybrook. In 1830 its attractions included its Irish lions born at Navan three weeks previously.[38]

This change in popular culture from the participatory and amateur such as footraces, what were termed 'rural pastimes', to the more commercial, organised activities can be seen quite clearly in the contrast between figure 3 from the late eighteenth century and those depicting the fairs of thirty or forty years later. The quiet, homely scene of Wheatley (figure 3), who visited the fair in the late 1700s is transformed into an elaborate, commercialised vista painted by Erskine Nicol, now in the Tate Gallery, London, who was in Dublin from 1845 to 1849. Freak shows arrived early; a contortionist, Levi Leach, put on a show at Donnybrook in 1815.[39]

In southern Europe the theatrical was at the centre of carnival, and for many the highlight of the pleasures of Donnybrook was a visit to a fit-up theatre. From the beginning of the nineteenth century the English fairs began to be dominated by the drama, although strolling players were by no means a new phenomenon. Itinerant entertainers began to add plays to their repetoire in the fifteenth century, or even drop altogether their juggling and tumbling in favour of play-acting. The first plays were religious mysteries, miracles and moralities.

In Ben Johnson's *Bartholomew Fair* a puppet showman asks a writer to simplify the story of Hero and Leander based on Marlowe's version, which he regarded as being too learned and poetical for his audience. London placenames were substituted for the original ones to make the Cockneys feel at home.[40] The substitution of the Thames for the Hellespont is reminis-

Figure 3 'Outside the Ale Tent at Donnybrook', Francis Wheatley
(1747-1801), ink and watercolour, National Gallery of Ireland

cent of the introduction of the Dodder into the story of the finding of
Moses in the song by Michael Moran, Dublin's famous Zozimus, a frequent visitor to Donnybrook, as we shall see later.[41]

By the time travelling theatres began to visit Donnybrook they were
very elaborate outfits indeed. The booths in which the performances took
place were barn-like structures constructed of wooden boards, tall and nar-
row in shape. External balconies were a common feature of these show-
booths throughout Europe, especially in France where they were most highly
developed. They eventually made their way to Donnybrook. On these barkers
strutted and actors paraded to draw the crowds as can be seen in Du Noyer's
sketch (figure 2). Trumpets blared and bells rang out, while harlequins perched
on the rail pointed to the show-cloth. Merry Andrews swapped banter with
clowns and grimaced, mimed, and pattered in soliloquy to the milling crowd
below.

On the Fair Green in 1828 Scott's Melodramatic Theatre 'raised its
gorgeous front' above all the theatres. The *dramatis personae*, male and female, attired in tawdry trappings, trimmed with tape and tinsel, tags and
tassels, were to be seen promenading the platform while clowns gamboled
and grimaced in order to gather the audience.[42]

Abridgements and adaptations were the lifeblood of the shows. *Hamlet* could be done in twenty minutes. The great favourite, however, was *Othello*, possibly because the character of the Moor was so easy to assume – a little soot did the trick. The owner of the booth would often stand at the side of the stage with a watch and cry out 'the time is up – commit the murder and down with the curtain.' The audience would then be ushered out and a new one brought in.[43]

Othello played at the Royal Hibernian Theatre on the Fair Green in 1844.[44] The most expensive seats cost two pence; these were the boxes and they had the luxury of straw on the seats. The pit cost a penny halfpenny, the rafters a penny, and if we are to believe the correspondent of *The Warder* it cost a halfpenny to little boys to peep through a hole in the roof, of which there was a selection of about 300. A novel effect was created by the smothering of Desdemona with a wisp of straw. The audience clamoured 'for her to be settled' in act 2 – in order to hear the actor who played the Moor sing the popular melody 'Take your time, Miss Lucy' before they were thrown out.

The man from *The Warder* then paid a visit to the nearby Mulligan's Dramatic Temple where *Hamlet* and *The Robbers of the Bloody Glen or The Miserable End of a Virtuous Washerwoman* were playing. In the latter the audience was treated to seven murders and a suicide in the last act. The pressman said that Miss Bridget Doran played the washerwoman to effect but that her agonies were too deep to be witnessed by a man of ordinary nerves, and he left at the conclusion of the first act.

A play seen by a visitor in 1824 began with the tinkle of a bell and the raising of a curtain which only half-concealed the stage. A dreadful-looking baron stepped forth in all the terrible dignity of a long black wig, short cloak, slashed hose, russet boots and spurs, all much used, and after him came the usual villain of the melodrama, and a convoluted plot ensued involving the conflagration of a castle and the accustomed happy ending with the union of two lovers. A comic scene, a pantomime – five minutes long –and a comic song concluded the entertainment, all within three quarters of an hour. They were then ushered out and a new audience entered.[45]

When a show began it was often found that the booth was so crowded that the front row would be under the actors' feet and it was not unusual for a scuffle to break out. Ten minutes was the duration of the show one was presented with if attracted by the name of a French company of comedians in 1823. It consisted of, in quick succession, a dance of savages, a Russian dwarf, and finally 'a pasteboard representation of His Majesty's Coronation'.[46]

The agents of official culture quickly disabused the fair-goers of any notion that they might have that the fun of the fair could impinge on the life of the city, as we have seen in the case of Foley, the carman.

The most immediate sequel to Donnybrook took place in the normally staid surroundings of the office of the B division of the Metropolitan Police in College Street. The board room, or court room of the College St. office was crowded every morning of fair week and the days succeeding it with a motley collection of people. Their condition was described in 1822:

> College St. – Donnybrook, being in this division, there were made of the occasion of the fair the customary number of complaints for broken heads, black eyes, bloody noses, squeezed hats, singed, cut and torn inexpressibles, jocks, and upper benjamins, loodies, frocks, tippets, reels and damaged Leghorns, together with sundry assaults, fibbings, cross buttocks, chancey lodgments, and ground floorings, too numerous to mention.[47]

A number of the actors from the penny theatres found themselves on the stage once again, not in a booth this time, but in the dock. They found it hard not to play to the gallery, and this led to two hilarious cases in 1838 and 1842. In 1838, in the Henry St. board room this time, what was described in the press as a 'tragedian', found himself one morning before magistrates Blacker and Duffy together with his colleague, Michael Moran, the well-known balladeer Zozimus, charged with being drunk and falling over a crippled man. The press correspondents revelled in scenes of this nature and took as much delight as the actors in transporting the boards of the theatre to the board room.

An unusual bustle was heard on the lobby of the court, it was reported, and a voice in lofty heroic measure was heard exclaiming – 'without a prompter, where will you that I go to answer this your charge'. 'This way, this way,' responded half a dozen of the new police, and John Browne, 'an unfortunate follower of the sock and buskin, was ushered in, in all the pomp of tragic distress.' He was in full theatricals and the black stain on his face led to the suspicion that he had been acting Othello.

Mr. Blacker asked what he had been charged with and a policeman replied 'why, your Worship, it appears that he had been at Donnybrook last night, performing at one of the three penny theatres, as a blacky-moor. He said that the cripple accosted them and hit him on the head with his crutch, saying 'down with Zozimus'. The magistrate fined Browne five shillings but as he said he had not got the money he was ordered to be brought off to prison.

He was then removed, but about half an hour afterwards he forwarded to the board room a petition setting forth the critical situation in which both himself and the public were likely to be placed. He was to appear in *Macbeth* that evening and he was sure that the audience would tear the house down at the non-production of their favourite. The magistrates, after some consideration, humanely remitted the penalty, and directed the prisoner's discharge.[48]

Release of tension also involved the playing of practical jokes, called 'larking' or 'roasting'; they especially became a real hazard to people who remained late at the fair. A common trick played on a newcomer to a tent was to leave one seat vacant which immediately collapsed as soon as he sat on it. It was not all laughing faces however. In 1833 six gentlemen who were dining in a tent, found, before the conclusion of the repast, that the tails of their coats had been cut off by some joker from the outside.[49]

In 1823 a dwarf had gathered a huge crowd by his antics to Brown's Equestrian Theatre. A wag thought he had got the better of him when he rushed up onto the stage and unceremoniously hurled him into the crowd. No injury was sustained and the dwarf resumed his station. Watching his chance however, he, some time later, caught the trickster off guard by rushing from the stage and giving him a 'remembrancer' under the chin. The chastened wag beat a hasty retreat.[50]

Many of the dupes were countrymen, recognized by their freize coats, but in 1824 every gentleman who was in any way unusually dressed became a target for pranksters and had to run a gauntlet in any tent they entered.[51] The numerous craftsmen and apprentices who went to the fair each year looked on it as a release from their very constrained everyday life. For these young people the sexual cycle of the year turned on these festivals.[52]

In 1779 a man and woman paraded naked on horseback through the streets of the city and then made their way to Donnybrook where they rode through the fair.[53] The whole exercise was done for a trifling wager. The *Freeman* said that such antics were 'of a very evil tendency and operate against morality and public decency'.

A common feature of the fair was a defrocked clergyman who set himself up and married, for a fee, any couple who presented themselves. The most famous of these was a renegade called the 'Tack'em', presumably because he tacked a couple together. This was a German clergyman, whose real name was Schultz and resided at Cullenswood Avenue, Rathmines. He married Dandyorum, a friend of Zozimus, and Peggy Baxter, known as 'Peg the Man'. In a lament for Donnybrook composed by John McCall in 1856 the 'Tack'em' is mentioned:

> The Sandymount gatherings are fled –
> Rathmines dance is knocked on the head
> And the Cullenswood tack'em is dead
> Who tied tight each pair from the fair.[54]

Samuel Lover has two of his characters, Peter and Biddy, visit Donnybrook Fair. Having imbibed their fill in a tent, between the allure of Biddy's eyes

and whiskey punch, Peter prevailed upon Biddy to go with him to a defrocked clergyman known as the 'Couple-Beggar', depicted by Lover in
figure 4.

> This high-priest of Hymen they found in a filthy hovel; he was all
> over dirt, snuff and whiskey; his spindle shanks seemed insufficient
> to support his bloated body; his knees bent inwards under the dis-
> eased incumbrance, and his carbuncled nose gave evidence that de-
> bauchery had reduced him to so disgusting a spectacle. When Peter
> and Biddy entered, he welcomed them with a drunken chuckle and
> went through a mumbled ceremony for half a crown.[55]

This type of quick marriage was a common affair at festivals. At Finglas the
winner of the smock-race, already alluded to, won a husband as well as a
smock:

> Oonagh e'er morn the sweets of wedlock tried,
> The smock she won a virgin, wore a bride.[56]

Some of those who made their matches at Donnybrook bided their time
and went home to their own parish priest to tie the knot. Barrington says

Figure 4 'The Couple Beggar of Donnybrook',
from a drawing by Samuel Lover, R.H.A.

that Father Kearny of Liffey Street – 'a good *clargy*' – told him that more
marriages were celebrated in Dublin the week after Donnybrook Fair than
in any two months during the rest of the year, and that it was gratifying to
see his young parishioners who had made their matches at Donnybrook go
back nostalgically there in a couple of years to buy whistles for their children.[57]

In Lysaght's song the fruits of 'Brookian love-making' are rather prompt:

> He meets with his Sheelagh, who, blushing a smile,
> Cries 'Get ye gone, Pat', yet consents all the while.
> To the priest soon they go; and nine months after that,
> A fine baby cries, 'How d'ye do, Pat,
> With his sprig of Shillelagh and Shamrock so green!'[58]

Sir Jonah Barrington was first introduced to 'The Brook' by his parents'
maidservants when he was a child. They would hie to the fair under the
pretence of diverting 'little master' and they and their sweethearts would
cram him with cakes so that he might not tell his grandmother what he saw.

A salutary warning was given to all those in the position of fathers and
brothers of young girls visiting the fair of 1829. It was said that any one of
them, if he viewed the fair with a scrutinizing eye, would have seen 'the coy
maid half willing to be pressed' go into a tent at perhaps seven or eight
o'clock, and 'thread the boards' with all the boldness of an experienced
courtezan.

It was not unknown, the journalist who issued the warning claimed,
that the father and mother of a fair daughter had gone to Donnybrook with
the most innocent of intentions, but met up with a clever debauchee whose
intention was to prise their daughter from them. He drew off the attention
of the father by first feeling his political pulse by praising O'Connell or
Cumberland, whichever suited. The mother was distracted in some other
way and the debauchee then 'poured that kind of poison into the ear of
their child which has led her into those paths from which she would never
again know the pleasures of a happy mind.'[59]

A parliamentary report on intoxication in 1834 corroborates what was
said of the danger to young women. C. Graves of the police Head Office in
his submission states that the occurrence of Donnybrook Fair every year
was regularly followed by a fresh supply to the streets of unfortunate young
women who owe their ruin to its intemperate orgies.[60]

Apart from the coy maid it appears that the fair ground was usually well
populated with women well advanced on those paths mentioned above.
John Keegan Casey, author *of The Rising of the Moon*, stated that he had read
such writers as Bulwer-Lytton and George Sand, but none of them had
prepared him for what he saw at Donnybrook. He spent two days and a part

of one night at the fair and he saw 40,000 females there and by five o'clock 30,000 of them were drunk.[61] A note of warning must be struck here however; at the time we speak of, as a general rule, any woman seen in a public place of leisure, unaccompanied by a husband or other suitable male, was regarded with suspicion. A member of a committee set up to suppress the fair in 1839 the Rev. W.B. Mathias, claimed that five-sixths of the inmates of the Magdalen Asylum owed their ruin to the fair.[62]

Instances of women resisting the advances of males and being forced into submission and raped are rare. An account of what was more than likely a rape comes from 1791. A young woman was taken to Mercer's Hospital in a 'mangled' state. She had been at the fair and was attacked by five or six villains, who then brought her to an adjoining place where she received shocking ill-treatment.[63]

An idea of how young girls were enticed into prostitution can be got from the experience of a young county Carlow girl in 1824.[64] The whole story first came to light when on the Saturday of fair week a young girl in a distressed condition was found in Trinity Street. She told the people who went to her assistance that her name was Anastatia Simmons and that she came from Tullow, county Carlow. She said that she had come with some people from that neighbourhood to Donnybrook Fair to sell cheese, of which she had purchased a small stock. On Saturday at the fair a man of respectable appearance, in the company of a fine-looking lady, came up to her and after some conversation told her that if she came to town he would immediately give her a place in his family, as he wanted a servant of her description. The lady and all her neighbours advised her to go. She decided to do so and she accordingly left with the pair. The gentleman, however, shortly after leaving the fair parted with the lady and brought her to a house in Dublin, and began to take liberties with her. When she realised what was going on she screamed and ran down the stairs, where two women below tried to hold her but she escaped, and was rescued by the passers-by on Trinity Street.

A sizable number of the ladies present on the Fair Green each year, especially in the evening, were hardened prostitutes. A number of the women would pick up clients at the fair and bring them back to their brothels in the city. An unnamed unfortunate young man met up with Margaret Brown, described as a low-sized, ordinary young woman, at the fair in 1834. He enjoyed the pleasure of her company at the fair and then adjourned with her to a house of suspicious character in town where he eventually fell asleep. When he awoke he found himself in a dire predicament as his clothes were nowhere to be found. His lady friend of the night then suggested that he would get them back if he paid for his night's lodgings.[65]

As opposed to the seamier side of love, the idealistic, romantic version remained important. A painting by William Brocas has as its centre-piece a radiant, loving couple, and Prince Pückler-Muskau finishes his description of the fair on a romantic note. He was charmed by a loving couple, excessively drunk, that he saw as he left the Fair Green:

> It was a rich treat to watch their behaviour. Both were horribly ugly but treated each other with the greatest tenderness and the most delicate attention. The love especially displayed a sort of chivalrous politeness. Nothing could be more gallant and at the same time more respectful ...[66]

According to Burke, another major theme of carnival, after food and sex, was violence.[67] Much of the violence, like the sex, was sublimated; in this case into ritual such as mock battles and cudgel play. However, the ritual was not always able to contain the violence and the revellers often went too far. In Basel in 1376 carnival turned into a massacre and in Bern in 1513 it became a peasant revolt, while May Day in 1517 in London turned into a riot against foreigners. Carnival at Romans in 1580, which has been the subject of an in-depth study by Ladurie, turned into a widespread massacr which ended with the peasants being hunted down and mercilessly killed.

In Ireland the name of Donnybrook has for long been a by-word for violence. Indeed the village, now an inner suburb of Dublin, bears one of the few Irish place-names to have given a word to the English language. The *Oxford English Dictionary* defines Donnybrook as 'a scene of uproar and disorder; a riotous or uproarious meeting; a heated argument.' Its use has been recorded in America and Australia and wherever English is spoken.[69]

An event which gave a word to the language must have attained mythic proportions, and a myth has grown up around Donnybrook Fair. It came to epitomise the gaiety of the Irish peasantry and their alleged fiery temperament which made them as ready to whack a head with a shillelagh as step out for a jig.

Charles O'Flaherty, writing on the fair of 1822, sums up this view of the pugnacious but lovable Irishman who 'will suddenly start a fight shouting 'every man for himself!' and give the person next to him, no matter who, a derry in the ear and the skirmish soon spreads with many the noses and hats included in the list of the wounded and missing, some of the owners of both being kilt.' An Irishman is the only man in the world who fights for amusement, he goes on to say. If he sees, something which was not very uncommon at Donnybrook, a fellow's head thrust through a hole in the tent, for the purpose of enjoying either a little fresh air, or the prospect around him, he is sure to hit it a crack, and he tells you that 'by his own sweet soul it looked so tempting that he couldn't resist the desire of giving it one tip!' The owner of the head on finding his father's son so ill-treated, generally collects his followers, then proceeds pursuant to ancient custom in search of the aggressor, who, in the interim had gathered 'a few boys', and the skirmish is in general terminated with shillelaghs on the banks of the Dodder.[70]

Barrington took up and popularised this jolly pugnacious Donnybrook myth. He says that a revolution had taken place in the Irish national character in his time and that it extended to sports and places of amusement like Donnybrook. Speaking, as he was, when the factions of the Liberty and Ormond, who used the fair to fight in the eighteenth century, were not much more than a memory, he says

> it is a mistake to suppose that Donnybrook was a remarkable place for fighting, or that much blood was ever drawn there. On the contrary it was a place of good humour. Men, to be sure, were knocked down now and then, but there was no malice in it. A head was often cut, but quickly tied up again. The women first parted the combatants and then became mediators; and every fray which commenced with a knock-down generally ended by shaking hands and the parties getting dead drunk together.[71]

Sir Jonah states that antagonists were very skilled in the use of the shillelagh, but it was only like sword-exercise and did not appear savage. Nobody was disfigured by it, he says, or rendered fit for a doctor. A cut on the skull was thought no more than the prick of a needle, and if they occurred they did not for a moment interrupt the song, dance and good humour.

Much of the violence at popular festivals was ritualised and carried out through the medium of stylised combat in this way, as Barrington seems to be suggesting, just as much of the sexual was expressed indirectly through double meaning verse and song. Corroborative evidence that ritual cudgel contests did take place at the fair is provided by the experience there of Philip Skelton, a Trinity student and later a well-known divine.[72] Skelton was in college from 1777 to 1781 and while there visited the fair. On the Fair Green a prize of a hat was set up for the best cudgel player and Skelton took up the challenge. Two cudgels with basket hilts were laid out for public view and Skelton lifted one and the other was taken up by a young man, a ring formed, and combat began, which Skelton won.

The myth was propagated in song and illustration (cudgel players are prominent, for example in figures 1 and 2. In Lysaght's song it is said of the typical visitor to the fair:

> He goes to a tent, and he spends half-a-crown,
> He meets with a friend and for love knocks him down
> With his sprig of Shillelagh and shamrock to green!
> At evening returning as homeward he goes,

His heart soft with whiskey, his head soft with blows
From a sprig of Shillelagh and shamrock so green![73]

From the reports of eye-witnesses which begin to appear in the newspapers
from the early 1700s, Donnybrook certainly lived up to its reputation as an
occasion for drunkenness, dissipation and violence. Earlier days are lost in
the mist of time but some indication that riot was a feature of the fair in the
1600s can be gained from an incident which happened in 1695 to a young
man who was to become a famous dramatist later in life.[74]

In that year George Farquhar, author of *The Beau Stratagem* and *The
Recruiting Officer* was a little less than a year attending Trinity College and
was awarded an exhibition amounting to £4 a year. He was involved,
however, with some other students in riotous behaviour in Donnybrook
Fair and his prize was immediately suspended; the authorities relented, however, in February of the following year and it was restored.

The popular conception of the fair as a battle-ground for faction fights is
true for the eighteenth century when two notorious factions took advantage of the large crowds that the fair presented to continue their old strug-
gle, and not generally for the nineteenth when the fair came to be regarded
in certain circles as a microcosm of Irish national character. A great deal of
violence certainly still took place up to the suppression of the fair in the
mid-nineteenth century but it was more the work of individual drunkards
or coteries of thieves and hooligans.

The commercial and social life of eighteenth century Dublin was often
disrupted by riot and tumult. The two factions that most often engaged in
these disturbances were the Liberty weavers on the south side and the Ormond
butchers on the north side of the Liffey. As well as the territorial rivalry the
enmity between the two groups had a sectarian complexion as the weavers
were Protestant and the butchers were, in general, Catholic.[75]

The annual fair of Donnybrook with its large gatherings of young apprentices from both areas provided an ideal opportunity for the old rivalry
to flourish. In 1737 a report appeared in the press which was very much in
keeping with the popular image of the gathering as a place of fighting for
the sheer joy of it: 'yesterday there was a great battle at Donnybrook Fair by
the Mob, who fought for the Pleasure of Fighting, in which many were
wounded, some of whom their lives are despair'd of.'[76] A subsequent report
gives us a clue to the nature of the trouble when it states that one of those
who sustained a gunshot wound in the skirmishes was in fact a butcher.

The seriousness of the rioting in 1750, when a 'most violent and outra-
geous fray' took place in which many limbs were lost, a constable by the
name of Mulligan badly injured, and a completely innocent and sick man
murdered on Donnybrook Road, caused a public outcry. Joseph Eason,
who was described as a sober, diligent man, had been ill with a fever and on

his recovery went to take the air on the road to Donnybrook. He strayed too near to the fair for his own good, however, and was murdered without any provocation by persons unknown.[77]

A law officer whose sober account of the violence and death at the fair strikes a chill note was the police magistrate, Frank Thorpe Porter. In his reminiscences he says that from boyhood he often visited the fair and could recollect many accidents and incidents of violence.[78] Indeed he believed that, for many years previous to its suppression, hardly a year passed without it being the cause directly or indirectly of lives lost.

He saw the body of a female taken out of the mill-race near the Fair Green, the woman having fallen in a state of intoxication. He also witnessed a furious encounter on Donnybrook bridge between coal-porters, a tough breed who often fought at the fair, and another gang, in which a man was thrown over the parapet and killed.

The worst experience he had there was in 1820, when an amiable and inoffensive young man named James Rogerson, who was walking beside him in the main street of the village at about eight o'clock in the evening, was struck on táhe head by a large stone thrown by a person unknown. The young man was knocked unconscious by the blow and when he had been revived a little Porter took him to his father's house in William St. where he died a few days later. The perpetrator was never found.

Eighteen-thirty-four was a particularly violent year with gangs of ruffians armed with crowbars and bludgeons in the early hours of the morning breaking into tents looking for money and attacking the employees and the proprietors. One tent-owner, who had enough, shot one of the attackers over the right eye and he died a short time later in Mercer's Hospital.[79]

The exuberance with which the carnivalesque was indulged in annually at the fair can be seen in the evidence above. Despite the difficulty of distinguishing the authentic voice of the man and woman on the Fair Green enough of the attitude of the common people to their festival filters through to see that it was a much anticipated annual social outlet for the people of Dublin and its hinterland. It is also clear that it was not confined to those at the bottom of the social ladder, but that a certain number of people of status and rank attended.

Lent Victorious

In the sixteenth century a concerted movement for the reform of popular culture began in the Christian churches. As the reformation gained ground and the Catholic counter-reformation in response to it fought back, popular culture came increasingly under attack.[1] The reason for this was that the gulf between the sacred and the profane during the middle ages was small, and so reform of the church necessarily meant reform of popular culture. This took the form of objections to a wide array of popular beliefs, practises and customs. It included such things as mystery plays, saints' days, pilgrimages, dancing, wakes, maypoles, magic and much more. The early attack came from the clergy and can be seen in Ireland in denunciation of wakes. A series of synods and provincial councils were held in all Catholic countries in the 1560s following the Council of Trent. In the archdioceses of Armagh and Tuam in 1660, and in Armagh again in 1668 and 1670 drinking at wakes was forbidden.[2]

By the time we have attitudes to Donnybrook Fair recorded a second wave of denunciation of popular culture was taking place; in this case the laity had joined the clergy as agents of reform.[3] Added to it was the spread of evangelicalism in English and Irish Protestantism from the mid-eighteenth century. The gulf between polite and popular culture began to widen.

The agents of official culture in Dublin who became increasingly hostile to the fair were the government, the municipal authorities, especially in the person of the lord mayor, employers and upper class gentlemen, especially those residing in the neighbourhood of the fair or along the route to it from the city; added to this was the police establishment and, of course, the clergy, both Catholic and Protestant. While the newspapers generally reflected the attitudes of these sections of society, who, it must be said, made up most of their readership, they could as we shall see sometimes take a wider view.

The view of the city's apprentices and tradesmen that the fair was an occasion of release was increasingly frowned upon by the city's employers and by the time we have views on it expressed in the newspapers – from the mid-eighteenth century on – it was seen by them as the resort of scoundrels, thieves, runaway apprentices and errant tradesmen. This was a time when many of the employers of apprentices had a paternalistic interest in their apprentices, not only controlling their working hours but their personal lives as well; the fact that many of them lived in made this much easier.[4]

The idleness that masters and other employers saw as a consequence of the fair was greatly resented. Some masters might have been willing to allow their apprentices to go for a day to the fair but often complained that it did not stop at that. They would only return out of necessity when all their own money, and all they could cadge from friends had been exhausted, and they were in danger of starving. In 1773 the *Freeman* complained that the fair encouraged idleness and intoxication among the lower orders and asked whether it could not be removed further from the capital city or whether recently imposed restrictions such as those imposed in London could not be imposed in Dublin.[5]

The economic consequences of such idleness among the working class was felt to be alarming. In putting forward its argument in 1777 the *Freeman* questioned the value of the economic gain to a few patent-holders and stall-keepers at Dublin's two major fairs when weighed against the amount of idleness induced:

> On a moderate calculation the number of tradesmen who are made idle by the fairs of Palmerstown and Donnybrook, it is computed that there is an annual loss to this city of twenty thousand pounds at least. It therefore becomes a question, whether there be a profit of superior value arising, on the other hand, to such individuals as are supposed to benefit by these public markets.[6]

In the very year, 1790, that Barrington visited the fair about which he wrote his enthuastic account, a condemnation appeared in the press which reflected the views of the city's employers and respectable businessmen. The *Freeman's journal* complained about 'how irksome it was to friends of the industry and well-being of Society to hear that upwards of 50,000 persons visited the fair on the previous Sunday, and returned to the city like intoxicated savages.'[7]

This view reflected the opinion that industriousness was the lynchpin of progress, a conviction which grew as economic development increased and the industrial revolution took hold. Coupled with this the rise of evangelicalism in the 1730s brought about a revival of the puritan emphasis on hard work, frugality and prudence.

The target of these attacks was the municipal authorities, embodied in the lord mayor, whom the press felt had the power to interfere effectively with the proceedings at Donnybrook. The fact was however that the Dublin civic authorities made a grave mistake in the 1690s when they parted with the ownership of the patent to the fair. The fair was now in effect private property which could not be legally wrested from the Madden family and only with caution proceeded against.

Apart from the idleness and drunkenness, violence was another worry for the press, no doubt reflecting the views of its elite readership. It continued its attacks on the lord mayor and in 1778 the *Dublin evening post* echoed the sentiments of the *Freeman* of the year before, after an affray at the fair left a man with his skull fractured and another with his leg broken.

It put it to the lord mayor whether the interests of a few tent keepers or the lives of His Majesty's subjects were of more value. It pointed out that at the previous year's fair a woman had been murdered nearby and appealed to the lord mayor to look after the lives and limbs of his children if he wished to be thought of as the father of the city.[8]

Could any of the agents of the new reforming culture see that the fair had a value as safety valve? In England popular festivals in which workers, masters and the gentry took part re-affirmed the cohesion of society and strengthened the moral economy.[9]

Dickens described Greenwich Fair as 'a periodical breaking out, we suppose, a sort of spring-rash: a three days' fever, which cools the blood for six months afterwards, and the extirpation of which London is restored to its old habits of plodding industry ... '.[10]

In some years press reports suggest that such a far-seeing view was held by a few and that the fair provided a safety valve for the working class through which dangerous frustrations arising from drudgery and poverty could be released in lateral aggression. A newspaper account of 1818 speaks of the sparkling glass circling round in a tent at Donnybrook:

> Thus the toil and labour of the working people of Dublin, for the year previous, is all forgotten in this scene of relaxation and instead of grumbling over their misfortunes, in sulky silence, they divert one another, by the relation of the fun they enjoyed, or the anticipation they will enjoy at Donnybrook Fair. While amusements of this kind are occasionally allowed to the lower orders, there is no fear of 'treason, stratagem and spoil' occupying their brains, and if there is a little bad blood in the way, 'a knock down for love' or a cut head lets it out entirely.[11]

This was not recognised by many and the call for the complete suppression of the fair, though an extreme one, was regularly called for by the press from the mid-eighteenth century on. The less drastic solution was the confining of the fair to just a couple of days, and especially discountenancing the sale of liquor there on the sabbath. This strategy was the one taken up by the lord mayor and the sheriffs, and officers in the regalia of the city were no strangers to the Fair Green in succeeding years. On the Friday of the fair week in 1765 the tents were pulled down by officers of the city but daringly re-erected on the Saturday. When Sheriff Hart heard this, he, together with a strong guard and about 25 cars went there and removed all the tents, as well as a collection of pots, tables and other items and carted them off to the Tholsel.[12]

The 1790s have been seen as a time when the 'moral economy', which had linked landlord and tenants in bonds of patronage and deference, gave way to a sharper, adversorial relationship as the impact of the French Revolution led to a greater class-consciousness.[13] In Ireland this led to the rebellion of 1798 and its murderous passions. With the outbreak of revolution in France hitherto innocent pastimes began to be looked on in a different light; the *Freeman's journal* stated

> Attempts to excite the spirit of tumult among the people is the concern of every man of respect and property in the kingdom. None else are concerned – the canaille have an interest in plunder and outrage. This is not like SHAM PIG-HUNTING, SHAM CUDGEL-PLAYING or FOOTBALL; a successful mob may proceed, by and by, like the French common people, to cutting off heads and burning houses – we are at present at profound peace in these kingdoms – accursed be the wretch who dare attempt to make it otherwise.[14]

As the 1790s progressed and the political and sectarian situation deteriorated large gatherings of the common people began to be seriously feared. This was not without good reason as the United Irishmen used sporting gatherings and communal festivals to spread their ideals;[15] with the spread of republican ideas from France there was no guarantee that the violence of the mob would be always turned on itself.

In 1798 itself the fair was allowed to go ahead, but a visit of the grenadier company of Liberty Rangers on Walking Sunday, who used the occasion for target-practice, was intended to intimidate. The fair was not allowed to run for long however for included in a number of emergency measures urged on the lord mayor by Castlereagh was the discontinuance of the assemblage at Donnybrook Fair.[16] By 1811 the political excitement had died down and the fair was crowded with English soldiers and the word Orangeman, said to be the only irritable subject then, was not heard all week.[17]

If the 1790s have been seen as a critical period for the withdrawal of the upper classes from popular culture[18] the evidence from Donnybrook would suggest that no great gulf opened up between classes in the first two decades of the nineteenth century.

Apart from distinguished visitors to Ireland who happened to be in Dublin during the time of the fair and visited it, such as Prince Pückler-Muskau[19] and the Grand Duke Michael, the youngest brother of Alexander, in 1818,[20] there is some evidence that the fair was patronised by the upper classes after the 1790s.

In the early years of the nineteenth century it was common for the corporation of Dublin to dine on the Fair Green. In 1819 they went to Cheever's Anchor Tavern Tent and dined there for the evening.[21]

On more than one occasion the fair was graced with the presence of the most distinguished person in the country, the lord lieutenant. According to Frank Thorpe Porter, the duke of Richmond as lord lieutenant in 1808, as well as being given to cock-fighting in Clarendon Street, attending cockle parties in Dollymount and visiting St. John's Well on pattern day, actually dined at Donnybrook.[22] In 1828, the Marquis of Anglesey, a very popular lord lieutenant who had been Wellington's commander of cavalry at Waterloo, visited the fair twice.[23] On the first occasion he had with him his three young sons and was received on the Fair Green with cheering and waving of hats and handkerchiefs. The noble visitor expressed himself highly gratified and returned for a second visit on the following day when permission was given for the fair to continue until the Thursday of the following week.

A depiction of the fair in 1830 by William Sadler in the National Library of Ireland, while obviously meant to be humorous, shows a wide cross-section of society present, from soldiers and academics to cudgel-wielders and mounted gentlemen.

While aristocratic and distinguished visitors made open and no doubt dignified visits to the Fair Green many people of respectability thought it better to keep their presence in a tent at Donnybrook a secret, especially members of superior ranks in the army who were frequent attenders. The journal *Paddy Kelly's budget* had eyes and ears everywhere and dutifully reported its findings to its readers after the fair of 1833. They thanked 'Old Sir Maxwell Wallace of the 5th Dragoons' for his custom in their tent despite being well muffled up in his military cloak.[24]

As the forces of respectability and morality began to grow in strength in the city after the Union and the spirit of the hard-drinking bucks and their lower class counterparts, the members of factions, was left behind, the middle and upper classes began to look upon the seemingly interminable festivities at Donnybrook as an annual affront to civilisation.

They met formidable opposition in Peter and John Madden. They stood firmly on the law in the form of their ancient patent, royally granted, and their opponents were at a loss as to how to get around it. They approached the matter of the complete suppression of the fair very gingerly. Most of them were property-owners themselves and recognised that the privilege granted to the Maddens was a form of private interest and should be touched with great reluctance. Much of their energies over the years was concentrated on limiting the fair to the number of days allowed by patent, and especially avoiding what they regarded as the desecration of the sabbath.

The problem was that the Maddens claimed that the patent allowed them fifteen days for the duration of the fair, which included two sabbath days. While the city fathers often tolerated the erection of tents on Walking Sunday, they usually ordered that they be struck before the following Sunday and very often took them down themselves and brought them to the Tholsel. But this depended on the lord mayor of the day – some exerted themselves and others did not.

The civic authorities took the unpopular step of interfering with Walking Sunday itself in 1807. The magistrates rode out and compelled people to strike their tents and take down fruit and other stalls. Even the *Freeman's journal*, which had taken a strong stand against the fair in previous years, was forced to complain: 'We cannot say we applaud this exercise of authority. No instance of this kind has ever occurred in London. God knows the recreations of the poor Irish are scanty enough and they ought to be suffered to enjoy the little enjoyment within their reach without molestation.'[25] In contrast 1814 was a lenient year and the fair was allowed to continue on the second Sunday without interference and the tents were not struck until the Monday.[26]

The view among many was that unless the civic powers took action the fair would have gone on for as long the lower orders had a penny in their pockets and until poverty forced them back to work once more. A practise grew up whereby on the payment of a sum of money for charity to the lord mayor, for the poor of Donnybrook or the Mendicity Institute say, he would allow the fair to continue well into the second week.

This practise enraged many of the wealthy businessmen and merchants living in villas in the area and they grew determined to curtail the nuisance of the fair as much as possible. In 1816, when £20 was paid by the tent-owners for the continuance of the fair a number of the residents in the area covering Donnybrook, Booterstown, Merrion Square and Leeson Street formed a pressure group called the Rathdown Association to organise opposition to the fair. Members of the association, of whom the La Touche banking family were the most prominent, decided to take decisive action against the fair of 1818.[27]

Whether the erection of tents and the gathering of people on the Fair Green constituted a violation of the sabbath was a matter of dispute, there was no doubt the sale of spirits on Sundays was against the law. The association engaged the services of the constable of the barony of Rathdown to buy spirits on the Fair Green on the sabbath and consequently a publican by the name of Brady was charged but the case was dismissed and the constable almost charged himself for buying spirits on Sunday![28] Despite a memorial from the association the following year to the lord lieutenant and the support of the police establishment the fair of 1819 was not interfered with either and the association quickly disappeared.[29]

This was the last occasion on which respectability was to be routed in such a comprehensive way. An inexorable cultural change was taking place in society which gradually began to enstrangle the fair. A new concern was abroad about the underlying basis of social stability. In Britain the solidarity of society was broken by the withdrawal in turn of the aristocracy, employers, articulate artisans and shopkeepers, and finally the politically conscious sections of the working class from many aspects of the older communal social life. This paved the way for a rash of abolitions of metropolitan fairs in the 1850s. Such a reforming spirit, reinforced by some peculiarly Irish forces which were unleashed at this time, spelt the beginning of the end for Donnybrook.

The annual fate of the fair continued to hinge on the attitude of the lord mayor. The man elected in 1824, Richard Smyth, was of sterner stuff than his predecessors and a strict sabbatarian. He was determined that the sabbath would not be violated during his tenure in office.

On 17 August, to the dismay of the upholders of the ancient rites of Donnybrook, Smyth issued a proclamation banning the erection of any structure of any kind at Donnybrook on Walking Sunday and the sabbath following. He would not turn a blind eye to the infringement of the law as his predecessors had done. His proclamation stated that 'custom which has heretofore prevailed of suffering the tents, booths etc. to be erected on the Saturday previous to the commencement of the annual fair day, hath uniformly caused the violation of the two successive Sabbaths, which is contrary to the law of these realms.'[30]

The proclamation went on to specifically forbid any tent, booth or receptacle for the sale of wine, spirits, ale, porter or any other liquors, or for the exhibition of wild beasts, horsemanship or theatrical performances to be erected on the Fair Green or adjoining ground before Monday 23 August and that all were to be removed on Saturday 29 August.

This move caused a storm of controversy in the city and engaged much public attention. It was reported on the nineteenth that the lord mayor had been occupied the previous two days in hearing the statements of several parties who conceived themselves aggrieved, and appeals began to mount asking him to rescind the proclamation altogether.[31]

Chief among the aggrieved were of course the Maddens. They rushed to the defence of their right to hold the fair for fifteen days including Sundays. This right was, they once more recited, handed down to them by ancient patent. They said that they had on several occasions conceded one Sunday to the wishes of the lord mayor, and were willing to do so in the present instance, but they denied his lordship's right to interfere.

Smyth replied by questioning the right of the Madden's to hold a fair for fifteen days at all. He said that if they could satisfy him, by the opinion of the law officers of the crown, that they had a right to hold a fair for fifteen days he would permit them to keep it for such time undisturbed, provided the sabbath was not infringed upon. If they had that right, he asked, why was a large sum of money paid over to one of his predecessors in office to permit the fair to extent to a second Sunday?

The matter was referred to the attorney general and in the meantime the Madden brothers memorialised the lord lieutenant. They pointed out that there 'was no institution known to the law in this country more ancient in its creation and uninterrupted in its continuance than the annual fair held in Donnybrook' granted by a charter of Edward I and held uninterruptedly ever since. They pointed out the importance of the fair in the national life which, they said, as a national amusement 'has long mixed with the recollections and habits of the people, and in some degree, associated with the character of the people'.

They put their case for allowing the traditional fifteen days claiming that if the lord mayor got his way they would be restricted to only four days considering that a day at the beginning and end of the week would be necessary to erect the tents and as the tent-holders had to travel long distances, many from England, this would prove impractical.

The lord lieutenant declined to become involved and referred the matter to the lord mayor and the result was that Smyth succeeded in curtailing the fair.[32] In order to be ready for the expected influx of visitors on the Monday the tent-holders held everything ready in the by-roads and lanes of Donnybrook on Sunday night and shortly after midnight the work of erection began by the glare of torches and the tented city arose, mushroom-like, to greet the pleasure-seekers on Monday morning. The toast of the week in the tents was said to be 'Conversion to the Lord Mayor!'

While the ban on Walking Sunday was not always strictly enforced in subsequent years, Smyth had shown the way and lord mayors in subsequent years kept a closer eye on the proceedings on Donnybrook Fair Green, often by his personal presence, as celebrated in verse in 1826:

> On he went, with his Tipstaves twain;
> In safety guarded himself and the chain;
> And long life to Lord Abbot, our valiant Mayor
> Who walked by daylight all round Donnybrook Fair.

The police establishment wished for the complete abolition of the fair and in the 1834 parliamentary report on drunkenness J.C. Graves of the head police office concluded his submission by stating that a great benefit would be conferred on the city and its vicinity by the abolition. He held out the example of the suppression of similar proceedings at St. John's Well some time previously but the fact that a royal charter was involved at Donnybrook he saw as the main stumbling block.[33]

Two years later Frederick Shaw, M.P. for Dublin University presented a petition from inhabitants of Dublin to the House of Commons.[34] Due to this pressure and a proclamation of the newly crowned Queen Victoria on the profanation of the sabbath the lord mayor of 1837, William Hodges, issued a proclamation not only banning the holding of the fair on Sundays but restricting the opening of tents selling alcohol to between the hours of nine in the morning and six in the evening. This effectively put an end to nights of carousing on the Fair Green as the fair of that year had a large police presence, and the establishment of the new Dublin Metropolitan Police saw to it that subsequent years were heavily policed also.

If Hodges, however, thought that he was shut of Donnybrook he was mistaken. No sooner was the fair over than sixteen of the booth-owners issued writs against him claiming that he had acted illegally. One, by a John Brady, was brought as a test case before the Court of Queen's Bench. The action of Hodges was vindicated and he won the case and was awarded costs. Brady declared himself a pauper, however, and Hodges had to sustain the high costs of £160. He wrote to the lord lieutenant pleading to be rendered harmless for his action in attempting to preserve moral decorum, but the request was refused out of hand and Hodges had to sustain the cost of his public spiritedness out of his own pocket.[35]

Eighteen-thirty-three was also the year in which Fr. Theobald Mathew joined the temperance movement in Cork. His subsequent mass movement coupled with O'Connell's call for self-control and discipline wrought a radical change all over Ireland. The evangelical movement which had been in existence for over a hundred years had little direct effect on Catholic Ireland, but through Fr. Mathew and O'Connell the virtues of sobriety, industriousness, prudence and frugality found an eager following the country.

Through the agency of the temperance movement and the repeal reading room a reformation of manners began to take place with a new emphasis on morality, family life and poor relief. Both in Ireland and England a gradual narrowing of what would be tolerated in public and an increasing tendency to suspect what was unregulated and unlicensed was taking place. The newspapers were to the forefront of this movement and they were increasingly finding allies in Dublin's successive lord mayors and the magistracy, zealous agents in ensuring that the new thresholds of public behaviour were not overstepped in the new policy. An increasingly Jansenist hierarchy and clergy were already seeing to it that the country patterns and wakes with their licentiousness and dissipation were suppressed or sanitised.

From 1838 on hardly a year went by without committees being formed in the city to call for the abolition of the fair. In 1839 the 'Donnybrook Committee' was chaired by Robert Guinness and subsequent abolition movements were often multidenominational; the Quaker humanitarian, James Haughton, and the Carmelite, Dr. John Spratt of Whitefriars' Street, joining forces in the attack. They harangued the fair-goers on their way to the Green from a platform in Donnybrook village in 1846 and 1847.[36] That the fair was continuing to be attended in large numbers can be seen from the 74,792 who attended in one day in 1841 according to a 'scientific calcula-tion' made by the Maddens.[37]

The dark year of 1847 had, ironically, substantial and well-stocked re-freshment tents, a revived 'Paddy Kelly' tent among them, which scoffed at the killjoys in the following advertisement:

Ye gentlemen all who are fond of rare fun
Rejoice with me now that our battle is won
And despite of teetotallers old Donnybrook Fair
(Long life to our erudite worthy Lord Mayor)
Will still be kept up – by the pen in my hand
Those men who would alter the laws of the land
And prevent some good fellows from having a spree
Should be kicked from Dunshaughlin to Donaghadee.[38]

The danger of such large numbers gathered at the fair enabling the spread of disease was often alluded to in the newspapers and when disease arrived once more in the city in the wake of the famine in 1849 the matter was raised again by middle class letter-writers to the papers. Their real motive being best pointed out by an anonymous correspondent who was described as an eminent physician in the city; this was the fear that disease would insinuate itself into affluent households through their Achilles heel – their servants: 'in former years none suffered but the perpetrators of those abomi-nations themselves. Now every drunken servant, whose excess at the Brook bring on him an attack of the disease, will import it into the family of which he is a member.'[39]

By the time the fair of 1850 came round the single individual who was regarded as the chief obstacle to any interference with the fair was removed by death and the way was cleared for the complete suppression of the fair. John Madden, the proprietor of Donnybrook Fair Green and the patentee of the fair was buried in the old graveyard of Donnybrook on 4 May 1850 aged 75 years.[40] For some years previous to his death he had become the sole defender to the family's right to hold the fair, as his brother Peter had died. John had no heirs and the patent passed into the hands of Eleanor, their sister. Another sister, Mary, had married a local grocer and publican, Patrick Dillon, and their son, Joseph, took up the task of running the fair with as much dogged determination as his uncle John and Eleanor seemed content to let matters rest in his hands.

A new arrival in the parish of Donnybrook in 1853 soon changed all that. Patrick J. Nowlan was appointed that year as curate in the Donny-

brook end of the combined Irishtown, Ringsend, Sandymount and Donnybrook parish. Fr. Nowlan had been ordained two years previously and
was a man of unbounded zeal and great energy who looked upon the annual orgy as a blot on the good name of the flock entrusted to his care and
was determined that the fair of 1854 would be the last. As a prominent
parishioner of his it did not take him long to acquaint himself with Eleanor
Madden and he soon became a close friend of the family to the point of
being appointed trustee of the family will.

We know from later reports that the movement which led to the buying
of the patent of the fair from Eleanor Madden started when an unnamed
gentleman in the area acquired the consent of Miss Madden to the sale. The
most likely candidate for this coup was either Joseph or Edward Wright of
Floraville, Donnybrook. These were two brothers of the family of that
name which had come to the area from Yorkshire and set up as hat-makers,
Beaver Row being named after the site of one of their factories. Both Joseph,
and Edward a barrister, joined with Fr. Nowlan in negotiations with Eleanor
Madden to end the fair.

Eleanor Madden was an old lady of a pious family and ill-equipped to
stand up to the persuasive promptings of a zealous young curate. The Madden family were always staunchly Catholic, but had resisted for decades the
moral pressure for the curtailment of the fair, even from their archbishop.
However the days of lay independence from the clergy were almost over
and John Madden was the last of that name to resist the will of the clergy.
Nowlan suggested that the time was ripe for the family to dispose of the
patent to the fair. This suggestion had been made before and a direct offer
was put to the family in 1842 when £6,000 was offered to them to relin-
quish their right, but as long as John Madden was alive there would be no
question of the offer being entertained.[41]

It is a tribute to Fr. Nowlan's and the Wrights' persuasive powers that
not only did she agree to sell the patent but they obtained it at the bargain
price of £3,000. With this agreement in hand, Wright and a number of
other influential people in the neighbourhood immediately went to the lord
mayor, Joseph Boyce, a man of like mind to their own.

The twilight of Donnybrook coincided with the demise of a large number
of fairs in England. In 1822 a new police act enabled the authorities there to
suppress illegal fairs or those running beyond their allotted time; if the title
to a fair proved unsatisfactory at petty sessions the fair was suppressed. This
efficient new instrument was used to suppressed fairs at Bow, Brook Green
and Stepney. Attempts to suppress Peckham and Camberwell failed in 1823,
the former being abolished in 1827 and Camberwell in 1855 when, in a
move similar to what had taken place at Donnybrook the right of the lord
of the manor was bought by a consortium, although in the English case the
fair green was turned into a public park.[42]

Bartholomew Fair still held sway in London although it was greatly curtailed, Greenwich being the other great fair at which Londoners disported themselves. 'Old Bartlemy' could be compared to Donnybrook, with which it had many remarkable coincidences. It was established around the same time as Donnybrook and was the great carnival of the people of London and the time of year at which it was held overlapped with that of Donnybrook. It was also in 1855 that its famous bells fell silent and the fair was abolished.

Previous attempts to interfere with Donnybrook Fair tended to be taken at the last minute and were usually too late. Boyce decided that as it looked as if their efforts would be successful at last he would move with alacrity. He called a meeting in the Mansion House on 14 May for the purpose of taking measures to abolish the fair. The meeting was attended by a wide cross section of the middle classes of the city and included a member of the aristocracy, George Nugent, the marquess of Westmeath. There was also a strong representation of both the Protestant and the Catholic clergy, and wealthy residents of the Donnybrook area and the road to it from the city.[43]

The lord mayor in the chair reminded his audience of their object, believing of course that they were not the kind of people who would be found at the fair but were not immune to its evil effects through their servants. He forestalled objections that people needed their recreations by stating that the railways provided a opportunity of going to other places and that from enquiries he had made the fair was not important any more for the sale of cattle or horses. A motion calling for the abolition of the fair was proposed by Nugent, seconded by Dr. Spratt and passed by the meeting and a subscription opened. By the end of the meeting Boyce was happy to announce that they had already a twelfth of the sum required and he felt sure that by the time of their next meeting, the following week, they would have the entire sum – a sanguine view indeed.

The abolitionists then addressed an appeal by circular to the 'Nobility, Clergy, Gentry, Merchants and Shopkeepers of the city of Dublin and its Vicinity' requesting their co-operation. Subscriptions could be left directly in the Mansion House or in a number of booksellers' shops in town. Those who wished to subscribe were asked to do so immediately as an answer had to be given to the patentees by 1 July.

The clergy of all denominations were quick to respond, including the Protestant archbishop of Dublin. The police commissioners and the military added their mite – Major General Falls stating that he was delighted to be able to remove such an occasion of temptation from the path of his men; what his men thought of the demise of one of their favourite haunts is not known. Edward Wright contributed a generous £100, members of the Pimm family £25 and various contributions were received from numerous city

businessmen such as Browne, Thomas & Co., T.M. Gresham and Thomas
Bewley.

As the summer advanced a number of collectors reported dissenting
voices; the loss of a place of recreation for the lower orders being the most
common. Nugent reported that Dr. Stokes of Trinity College, on making
his contribution, said that he hoped that the abolition of the fair would be
offset by the opening of alternatives for the lower orders. This matter was
discussed briefly by the abolition committee who thought that it would be
possible to open St. Stephen's Green more widely to the public.[44]

More subscriptions were received including that of a William Baxter of
Grafton Street, whose workers had willingly agreed to pay one shilling each
to have the temptation removed from themselves and their children. But
while the subscriptions began to slow down in July and the committee
discussed the idea of employing paid collectors they had good news on the
legal front. Their council advised that he had looked into the title of Miss
Madden to the tolls and emoluments of the fair and found it in order.[45]

However, both Miss Madden and the committee must have been dis-
mayed to read a proclamation which appeared in conspicuous places in the
vicinity of Donnybrook in the middle of July. This was headed 'Important
to the Public – Donnybrook Fair' and was signed by Joseph Dillon. In it he
stated that as the time for holding the fair was drawing near he was now
apportioning places on his land in Donnybrook to respectable parties for
theatrical amusements and the like as he had done annually for upwards of
thirty years. Dillon adroitly summoned to his cause religious grievance and
popular democratic feeling alike. He pointed out that the fair was established by royal charter and as it had not been repealed by any parliament the
people in law could hold their fair as usual. This was notwithstanding the
fact that the previous year an attempt was made, under the guise of dimin-
ishing crime, to set up two proselytizing centres where the faith of the
children of poor Catholics had been tampered with for the wretched consideration of a little soup, some bread, apples and stirabout which had been
sparingly dealt out to them.

He continued on this highly sectarian note by saying that it was believed
generally in Donnybrook that if there was even one licensed Protestant
publican or grocer in it that many of those who in vain sought the annihi-
lation of the fair would be found battling for the common rights of that
solitary individual. He took up the case of the honest carmen who were
deprived of their rights, against the proprietors of the Kingstown railway
who had made £2,000 by a cheap trip to Kingstown – on the sabbath day.
This had left the poor carmen idle and had filled the coffers of quakers,
'laying the whole village of Donnybrook a waste or wilderness wherein for
soupers to howl and do their work of devastation among the populace.'

After his signature he made sure to point out that he was the nephew of the late John Madden who had owned the Fair Green.

This notice, not surprisingly, came to the attention of the metropolitan police and they sought advice as to what extent they could interfere with the holding of the proposed fair. The Attorney General gave his opinion in August, and it proved that Dillon was quite right – the buying of the patent was not enough to put an end to the fair; it could go ahead as long as the law was not violated. While he regarded the proclamation as highly objectional he believed that all the abolitionists could do was to appeal to the public not to visit the locality. He recommended that the Madden family make it clear that they would not permit the fair or any trespass on the Fair Green and that the drinking and public order laws would be strictly enforced.

In pursuance of this advice the solicitor for the trustees of the patent holders placed a notice in the press stating that despite public advertisement to the contrary no fair would be held that year and that any attempt to hold the fair would be illegal – not quite what the Attorney General had said – and that the police would take all necessary steps to prevent any violation of the law and to make all parties who attempted it amenable to justice. The police also notified the public that no crowd would be allowed assemble on the Fair Green. Dillon had published a statement in the press on behalf of himself and sixty-three named inhabitants of Donnybrook and its vicinity saying that they would do their utmost within the law 'in common with the rights and interests of the poor of the locality' to sustain their own interests by accommodating the inhabitants of Dublin during fair week with refreshments and amusements of every description. They were confident that the fair would take place to the advantage of several hundred of the working people of the town.[46]

Dillon's fair proceeded. On Walking Sunday a large assemblage gathered in the field behind his public house. At one end of it a number of tents had been erected and at the other end more were in course of construction. Cakes, refreshments and toys for the children could be bought at numerous standings. Strewn throughout the field were the various bits of merry-go-rounds, swings and other amusements ready to be erected. It was reported that several outside cars drove along the road through the old fair green but the only sight that met their curious gaze was a large herd of grazing cattle. Over a hundred police were deployed in the area under the command of head superintendent Monaghan.[47] Joseph Dillon claimed that about twelve thousand people of rank and respectability, as he put it, visited the locality during the week and that several horses, cows and sheep had been sold at the fair.

Dillon and his supporters in thanking the people of Dublin for their support despite 'the terrorism and police tyranny on the highway' which had consisted of shoving people about and stopping cars and returning cars to the city. They scoffed at the idea of providing alternative amusements such as railway excursions, 'the rich *treat* of sitting in a third class carriage in the dark all the way home!', and warned that when town council elections came round the people would dispose as they saw fit of those in power who ruled in such an arbitrary way.

Dillon had put his finger on the kernel of the issue when he stated that the charter remained unrepealed. The indenture handing the tolls and customs over to the abolition committee stated that it would enable the government by a legislative enactment to end the fair. This had not been done and so for many years to come Joseph Dillon was able to hold his version of the fair in his field. The advantage of such an arrangement was that because it was private property no uniformed police could enter it without good reason.

As regards the wishes of enemies of the fair that alternatives for the citizens to the debauchery of Donnybrook be provided, it came to nothing. A number of private concerns did use the name of Donnybrook to advertise alternative amusement for people, but this was a case of cashing in on the name rather than any philanthropic concern for their fellow man. The Royal Portobello Gardens regularly used the name of 'Donnybrook Fair Week' to attract a crowd to its entertainments such as pony races in 1857.

'Terry Driscoll', a humorous columnist of *The Warder* was forced to ask in 1856

> where's the substitute for poor oul' Donnybrook? I thought, provided we promised to behave ourselves properly, and be as amaynable to the pious and the police as little boys are to a stern schoolmasther when he ordhers 'em to use their pocket hankitchers and hould up their heads, that we wor to have public gardens in lieu of public-houses, or amusement in some shape for the million![48]

Much to the annoyance of the authorities Dillon, with the help of his daughter Eliza, continued to hold a fair on his premises annually, although closely watched by the police. In 1859 it became necessary for the Dillons to obtain a certificate necessary to acquire a renewal of their license, and the police decided to oppose it.

On 9 November, 1859 the case came before the magistrates in College Street police office, the scene of so many hilarious epilogues to the fair over the years. Mr. Stronge, one the magistrates, said that the certificate that they had the power of granting was to the effect that the public house was well conducted and that the owner was a person of good character. Miss Eliza Dillon of Donnybrook was the applicant and it was opposed by Mr. Mahon police superintendent.[49]

The police contended that Miss Dillon had set up the fair on a new site, where she had allowed booths to be set up in which spirits and other drink had been sold. During the last fair they said that it was frequented by people of the worst character and was a scene of riot and disorder – people had been assaulted and their hats had been knocked off. They further stated that no animals had been sold except two donkeys, which had been bought by Miss Dillon. Miss Dillon in reply stated that she was not responsible for the conduct of people in the field as it was not included in the house and premises for which she had a license.

Mr. Stronge said that as Miss Dillon had sold spirits in the booths on the field up to eleven at night it was clear that she had a license to do so and that in a previous court case when summons had been brought by the police against people for selling spirits she had stated that spirits were sold on the field on her directions. On these grounds the summons were dismissed. The fact that the license applied to the field had been proven by herself and now she wished to state that the field was not included in the license. It was the opinion of the magistrates that Miss Dillon had not conducted the area covered by her license in a fit manner and the certificate was refused.

When an appeal by the Dillons to the recorder failed the Dillons began to lay plans to circumvent this obstacle and hold a fair in 1860. It came to the notice of the police that the Dillons intended to apply for a spirit grocer's license; this allowed them to sell drink to be consumed elsewhere but they believed that they were banking on the fair being over before the police could act against them. The police were aware that it was unusual for the inland revenue authorities to refuse such a license if the applicant pursued it, but they pleaded that in this case it be refused. They stated, and were backed up by the Lord Lieutenant, that the circumstances were such in this case that it was necessary for the public good that it be refused. When the revenue authorities in Somerset House stood firm the police pointed out to them that all that was necessary was that the license be delayed until after 26 August and this they agreed to do.[50]

While the temporal powers were garnering their forces against Mr. Dillon and his daughter the spiritual authorities decided to weigh in. The Catholic archbishop of Dublin, Paul Cullen, penned a pastoral letter to be read at masses and vespers in the churches of the archdiocese on Sunday, 15 August and the Sunday following. He reminded his flock that some years before the lord mayor of the day and very many citizens of every class and every religion had made great efforts and considerable pecuniary sacrifices to put a stop to the revolting scenes of drunkenness and degrading immorality which were enacted every August at Donnybrook and that a great deal of sin and public scandal had thus been averted.[51]

He went on to state that it was regretted that some persons were said to be preparing to restore the former state of things and ' for the sake of some temporal advantage to expose to the danger of sin and of eternal ruin many souls that have been redeemed by the precious blood of Jesus Christ.' Under these circumstances he asked his priests to warn their people about the dangers present 'at the disgraceful scenes of which Donnybrook is attempted to be the theatre.'

Despite these strong condemnations of their church, which was gaining in power and prestige in Ireland by the year, Joseph Dillon and his daughter, in the spirit of their uncle, John Madden were not daunted nor was their resourcefulness exhausted. On the Tuesday before Walking Sunday, the acting collector of inland revenue in Ireland wrote to his superiors in London asking if the prohibition on the Dillons extended to a beer license as well as that of a spirit grocer, as he had been informed that Dillons daughter was to make an application for a beer license. A flurry of correspondence between Dublin and London resulted in the license being refused.

Dillon opened his field on Walking Sunday with a few shaky-looking awnings and dismal-looking tents, but due to the pressure from the clergy and the restrictions on the sale of liquor very few turned up and although it picked up during the week numbers were very much down on previous years causing the press to declare the demise of the fair.

The small group of zealous reformers who had spearheaded the abolition movement were very disappointed that the legislative enactment that they felt they had paved the way for had not materialised. The government was now however looking at the whole question of fairs and markets in Ireland and they felt that legislation was long overdue. During the debate on the question it was stated that there were 1,297 fairs held annually in Ireland and that only 488 of them kept strictly to patent. To redress this and other abuses a fairs' and markets' bill had been introduced in parliament in 1858 and 1859. Due to pressure from Spratt and the abolitionist body a clause was introduced stating that owners had to come forward and prove their titles in law or face a £200 fine for holding an illegal fair.

The debate was still dragging on in 1862 without any legislation being passed and when a fairs' and markets' bill came up for discussion that year Lord Naas referred to clause 36, the inspiration of Nowlan and Spratt which was 'directed at the suppression of nuisances, such as those arising from the remnants and dregs of that classic celebrity, Donnybrook Fair.' It was intended to abolish fairs held illegally and where it was the unanimous wish of everyone in the locality that they should be abolished. When Robert Peel rose to speak he said that he was sorry to hear that a lady was the owner of the Fair of Donnybrook, and that he hoped that she did not think him ungallant but that he must really insist that she hold no more fairs there. This caused great laughter in the house, the members obviously aware of the reputation of Donnybrook.[52]

The Dillons knew that it was vital to the survival of the revived fair that liquor, whether in the form of spirits or beer, be available in the field. The ruse that they used in subsequent years was to get other publicans to apply for a license to sell on the field during the week. To the dismay and surprise of the Dublin authorities this succeeded and Dillon got some of 'his numerous friends' in Dublin to whom he often appealed for support in his posters to ply their trade in his field; in 1862 Thomas Patterson of Marrowbone Lane, James Fitzpatrick of North King Street and Daniel Chapman of Barrack Street traded there on the strength of their licenses.[53]

So matters continued until the momentous year of 1866. It was decided that the new Catholic church which was to open in Donnybrook would be dedicated to the Sacred Heart in reparation for all the sins committed on the Fair Green over the centuries. A site on the far side of the Dodder was chosen as it overlooked the scene of ancient infamy. To symbolise the victory of virtue over vice there was only one date on which the grand and solemn opening of the church could take place – Walking Sunday of time immemorial, the Sunday immediately preceding 26 August or on which the 26th fell, and propitiously enough it fell on a Sunday in 1866.[54]

Joseph Dillon knew that something special would be needed in 1866 to compete with the pomp and ceremony of a gala occasion in the life of the resurgent Irish church, made all the more special by the fact that it would be the first major event to be presided over by the newly-created Cardinal Cullen, the first such in Irish history. Cullen had taken a special interest in the progress of the Donnybrook church and had visited the site.

Dillon began to search for some novelty which would attract the crowds to his field. What was called 'pedestrianism' was all the craze in Britain at this time and Dillon succeeded in engaging a lady known as 'The Great Pedestrian' to come to Donnybrook and put on a display of endurance – she would walk 1000 miles in as many consecutive hours. In order to achieve this she came to the village three weeks before Walking Sunday and commenced to walk day and night non-stop. As the lady walker kept up her efforts the decorators were putting the finishing touches to the new church.

The great day began in Donnybrook when Joseph Dillon opened his field attached to his public house at the entrance to the village at nine in the morning. The crowds were already gathering for the dedication of the church, the lucky ones with their tickets for pews inside in their hands, the others content to gaze outside. Among them, arriving from the city, was a less respectable breed. A large contingent of gamblers, many of them trying in vain to hide their wheels of fortunes, mingled with the pious, and stopped off at Dillon's field. Many of the church goers cast curious glances at the field with its one miserable spirit tent as they hurried past to the ceremony.

Proceedings began with the arrival of the cardinal archbishop shortly after eleven o'clock. He was saved an embarrassing view of the fair ground as he passed by in a closed carriage. He was joined in the church by two bishops, the lord mayor of Dublin and the leading Catholics of the city. The sermon was preached by the Very Rev. Thomas Burke O.P., one of the most famous preachers of the day. His text was 'No man can serve two masters' and it was not long before he made the anticipated reference to the fair. He said that for many a long year the place at which they were assembled was the special inheritance and possession of the Evil One: 'hither came souls in the first beauty of their innocence or in the restored robe of repentance to lose grace and purity and to draw down upon them the awful anger and curse of God', he boomed. 'But joy there would be in the church of Donnybrook amongst the angels of God. The reign of the Lamb had come – the old enemy, the Great Dragon, seducer of souls was cast out.' The ceremony lasted until after two o'clock and the cardinal was cheered by the large crowd now assembled on his way out.[55]

Joseph Dillon was greatly disappointed that all his efforts bore little fruit – his field was frequented by small numbers and closed after three days, and he confessed to Inspector Dowling of the police that he now regretted ever having attempted to uphold the fair and would never try again. The old battler had succumbed to the overwhelming forces of church and state ranged against him. True to his word he did not open his field in 1867 but a neighbouring publican, John Lawlor, who had supported Dillon in the past, opened one attached to his premises and did a little business.

So we come to the last attempt to revive the glories of 'The Brook' and miserable indeed it proved to be. Once again the Dillon family entered the fray after their absence in 1867, but without Joseph Dillon. The stalwart in the fight for the ancient rights had died in the intervening year. His widow, perhaps hoping to improve her financial position after the loss of her husband and learning that John Lawlor was not interested, decided to open for business in 1868.

About 120 people turned up on Walking Sunday 'of the lowest class', according to the police, and about the same number were entertained for the next three days by a penny theatre and some tumblers, but by Wednesday the field was deserted. No music was heard in the licensed premises of the town, an important factor in the failure of the fair in the eyes of the police.[56]

So ended ignominiously the great fair of Donnybrook, for neither the Dillons nor Lawlor opened their fields to the public again. The great national institution, a pale shadow of its former glory after its tortuous death throes of the previous thirteen years, passed into the folk memory.

Notes

An. rec. Dub.	J.R. Gilbert (ed), *Calendar of ancient records of Dublin* (Dublin 1889-1944), 19 vols.
C.S.O.R.P.	Chief Secretary's Office, registered papers
D.E.M.	*Dublin evening mail*
D.E.P.	*Dublin evening post*
F. J.	*Freeman's journal*
J.S.R.A.I.	*Journal of the Royal Society of Antiquaries of Ireland*
N.A.	National Archives, Dublin
S.N.	*Saunder's newsletter*

INTRODUCTION AND HISTORICAL BACKGROUND

1 *F.J.* 26/8/1829.

2 Peter Burke, *Popular culture in early modern Europe* (London, 1978), chap. 7, 'The world of Carnival', pp. 178-204.

3 Burke, *Popular culture*, pp. 191-9.

4 Burke, chap 8, 'The Triumph of Lent'.

5 B.H. Blacker, *Brief sketches of the parishes of Donnybrook and Booterstown* (Dublin, 1861).

6 William Addison, *English fairs and markets* (London, 1953).

7 Henry Morley, *Memoirs of Bartholomew Fair* (London, 1859).

8 J.T. Gilbert, *Historical and municipal documents of Ireland* (London, 1870), p. 61.

9 Addison, *English fairs and markets*, p. 10.

10 Addison, *English fairs and markets*, p. 10.

11 Charles Doherty, 'Exchange and trade in early medieval Ireland', in *J.R.S.A.I*, cx (1980), pp. 67-89.

12 Gilbert, *Historical and municipal documents*, p. 51.

13 Addison, *English fairs and markets*, p. 10.

14 Francis Elrington Ball, *A history of the county Dublin* part 2 (Dublin, 1903) pp. 48-63.

15 James Todd (ed.), *The martyrology of Donegal – a calendar of the saints of Ireland*, translated by John O'Donovan (Dublin, 1864), p. 264.

16 Doherty, 'Exchange and trade', p. 81.

17 Charles Doherty, 'The monastic town in early medieval Ireland', in H.B. Clarke and Angrett Simms (eds) *The comparative history of urban origins in non-Roman Europe*, (Oxford, 1985), pp. 80-3.

18 Keith Thomas, *Religion and the decline of magic* (London, 1971), p. 54.

19 Addison, *English fairs and markets*, p. 6.

20 Maire MacNeill, *The festival of Lughnasa* (2 vols., Dublin, 1913).

21 Edward Gwynn, *The metrical dinnshenchas*, part 3 (Dublin, 1913), p. 25.

22 *Report of the select committee appointed to inquire into … intoxication among the labouring classes*, H.C., 1834 (559), VIII, 315, p. 442, letter from Greaves.

23 Gilbert, *Historical and municipal documents*, p. 62 and Blacker, *Brief sketches*, p. 46.

24 Blacker, *Brief sketches*, p. 46.

25 Gilbert, *Historical and municipal documents*, p. 189.

26 Blacker, *Brief sketches*, p. 46.

27 Blacker, *Brief sketches*, p. 59.

28 Ball, *History of county Dublin*, pt 2, p. 50 and Blacker, *Brief sketches*, p. 59.

29 Ball, *History of county Dublin*, pt 2, p. 50 and Blacker, *Brief sketches*, p.110.

30 Blacker, *Brief sketches*, p. 47.

31 *Anc. rec. Dub.*, vi., p. 192.

32 Blacker, *Brief sketches*, p. 76.

33 Blacker, *Brief sketches*, p. 47.

34 Monument in Donnybrook graveyard, in Danny Parkinson, *Donnybrook graveyard* (Dublin, 1993).

35 R.J Kelly, 'Donnybrook, origin of name – it's famous fair' in *J.R.S.A.I*, xliv (1919), p. 141.

36 N.A.,Official Papers, 1832/531, return of J.& P Madden to Sir William Gossett.

37 John Cantwell, *Practical treatice on the laws of tolls and customs*, (Dublin, 1817), p.17.

38 Department of Irish folklore, University College Dublin, Dunton's letters, letter 7, p.116.

39 *The Warder*, 28/8/1841.

THE WORLD OF CARNIVAL

1   Burke, *Popular culture*, pp. 191-2.

2   Burke, *Popular culture*, pp. 195-6.

3   Burke, *Popular culture*, p. 3.

4   E.P. Thompson, *Customs in common* (London, 1991), p. 5.

5   Burke, *Popular culture*, p. 179.

6   E. Le Roy Ladurie, *Carnival at Romans* (Harmondsworth, 1981), ch. 12; Burke, *Popular culture*, pp. 179-99; Douglas A. Reid, 'Interpreting the festival calendar: wakes and fairs as carnivals' in R.D. Storch (ed.), *Popular custom in nineteenth century England* (London, 1982), pp. 124-53.

7   Thomas Crofton Croker, *The popular songs of Ireland* (London, 1839), pp. 116-17.

8   'The Humours of Donnybrook' in James N. Healy (ed.), *The Mercier book of old Irish street ballads*, III (Cork, 1969), p. 34.

9   *S.N.* 27/8/1823.

10 *Paddy Kelly's budget*, 4/9/1833.

11 *F.J.*, 26/8/1820

12 Patrick Myler, *Regency rogue, Dan Donnelly, his life and legends* (Dublin, 1976), p. 118.

13 *S.N.*, 30/8/1815.

14 Frank Thorpe Porter, *Gleanings and reminiscences* (Dublin, 1875), pp. 349-55.

15 *S.N.*, 26/8/1822.

16 *F.J.*, 25/8/1823.

17 *Paddy Kelly's budget*, 4/9/1833.

18 *S.N.*, 28/8/1821.

19 *S.N.*, 25/8/1824.

20 Herman Pückler-Muskau, *Tour in England, Ireland & France in 1828 and 1829* (2 vols. London 1832) i, pp. 203-5.

21 *F.J.*, 25/8/1823.

22 *Paddy Kelly's budget*, 27/8/34.

23 B.P. Bowen, 'Dublin humorous magazines' in *Dublin historical record*, xiii, no. 1, (March-May 1952), pp. 2-11.

24 *Paddy Kelly's budget*, 27/8/1834.

25 *True salmagundi*, 23/8/1834.

26 Burke, *Popular culture*, p. 184.

27 Croker, *Popular songs*, pp. 116-17.

28 Patrick Fagan, *The second city: portrait of Dublin: 1700-1760* (Dublin 1986), p. 85.

29 *S.N.*, 30/8/1815.

30 Seán Ó Súilleabháin, *Irish wake amusements* (Cork, 1969), p. 96.

31 *S.N.* , 30/8/1815.

32 Jonah Barrington, *Personal sketches of his own time* (3 vols, 3rd edition, London, 1869), ii, pp. 334-8.

33 Often so named in the newspapers and journals, e.g. *Paddy Kelly's budget*, 4/9/1833.

34 *F.J.*, 4/9/1811.

35 Barrington, *Personal sketches*, ii, p. 241.

36 *F.J.*, 28/8/1812.

37 *Carrick's morning post*, 25/8/1819.

38 *S.N.*, 27/8/1830.

39 *Carrick's morning post*, 2/9/1815.

40 Ben Jonson, *Five Plays* (Oxford, 1980), p. 587.

41 Gulielimus Dubliniensis Humoriensis, *Memoir of the great original Zozimus* (Dublin, 1871), p. 21.

42 *F.J.*, 31/8/1828.

43 James Grant, *Penny theatres from sketches in London 1832* (London, 1952) p. 19.

44 *The Warder*, 31/8/1844.

45 *Dublin university magazine*, Oct. 1861.

46 *S.N.*, 27/8/1823.

47 *S.N.*, 28/8/1822.

48 *F.J.*, 3/9/1838.

49 *S.N.*, 29/8/1833.

50 *Faulkner's Dublin journal*, 29/8/1823.

51 *S.N.*, 28/8/1824.

52 Thompson, *Customs in common*, p. 51.

53 *F.J.*, 26/8/1779.

54 P.J. McCall, 'Zozimus' in *Dublin historical record*, vii (1945), pp. 135-49.

55 Samuel Lover, *Further stories of Ireland*, ed. D.J. O'Donoghue (London, 1899), pp. 58-62.

56 Fagan, *Second city*, p. 85.
57 Barrington, *Personal Sketches*, ii, p. 240.
58 Croker, *Popular songs*, pp. 116-17.
59 *S.N.*, 24/8/1829.
60 *Select committee report on intoxication*, letter of Graves, p. 442.
61 Benedict Kiely, *Dublin* (Oxford, 1983).
62 *The Warder*, 3/8/1839.
63 *F.J.*, 6/9/1791.
64 *S.N.*, 31/8/1824.
65 *F.J.*, 3/9/1834.
66 Pückler-Muskau, *Tour*, i, pp. 203-5.
67 Burke, *Popular culture*, p. 186.
68 Ladurie, *Carnival at Romans*.
69 Eric Partridge, *A dictionary of slang and unconventional English*, Paul Beale, d. (eighth edition, London, 1984), p. 328.
70 Rory O'Reilly [Charles O'Flaherty], *Retrospection* (Dublin, 1824), pp. 87-8.
71 Barrington, *Personal sketches*, ii, p. 333.
72 Samuel Burdy, *The life of Philip Skelton* (Oxford, 1792), pp. 20-1.
73 Croker, *Popular songs*, pp. 116-17.
74 A.J. Farmer, *George Farquar* (London, 1966), p. 8.
75 John Edward Walsh, *Ireland sixty years ago* (Dublin, 1847); Fagan, *Second city*, pp. 47-9; Sean Murphy, 'Municipal politics and popular disturbances: 1660-1800' in Art Cosgrove (ed.), *Dublin through the ages* (Dublin, 1988), pp. 77-92.
76 *The Dublin daily post and general advertiser*, 16/8/1737.
77 *F.J.*, 25-8/8/1750.
78 Porter, *Gleanings and reminiscences*, pp. 350-1.
79 *S.N.*, 1/9/1834.

LENT VICTORIOUS

1 Burke, *Popular culture*, chap. 8, 'The triumph of Lent', pp. 207-43.
2 Ó Súilleabháin, *Irish wake amusements*, pp. 19-23.
3 Burke, *Popular culture*, pp. 234-43.
4 Thompson, *Customs in common*, p. 36.
5 *F.J.*, 31/8/1773.
6 *F.J.*, 2-4/9/1777.
7 *F.J.*, 31/8/1778.
8 *D.E.P.*, 27/8/1778.
9 Thompson, *Customs in common*, p. 47.
10 Charles Dickens, *Sketches by Boz*, 'Greenwich fair' (Oxford illustrated edition, Oxford, 1969), p. 112.
11 *S.N.*, 29/8/1818.
12 *Faulkner's journal*, 3/9/1765.
13 Kevin Whelan, 'The United Irishmen, the enlightenment and popular culture' in David Dickson, Dáire Keogh & Kevin Whelan (eds), *The United Irishmen: republicanism, radicalism and rebellion* (Dublin, 1993), pp. 276-90; Kevin Whelan, 'The geography of hurling in Ireland' in *History Ireland*, i, no. 1 (Spring, 1993), pp. 27-31.
14 *F.J.*, 22/8/1789.
15 K. Whelan, 'The United Irishmen' in Dickson et al., *The United Irishmen*, p. 297.
16 *F.J.*, 1/9/1798.
17 *F.J.*, 4/9/1811.
18 Wheelan, 'The United Irishmen', pp. 294-6.
19 Pückler-Muskau, *Tour*, I, pp. 203-5.
20 *S.N.*, 29/8/1818.
21 *Carrick's morning post*, 30/8/1819.
22 Porter, *Gleanings and reminiscences*, p. 351.
23 *F.J.*, 29/8/1828.
24 *Paddy Kelly's budget*, 4/9/1833.
25 *F.J.*, 24/8/1807.
26 *S.N.*, 1/9/1814.
27 *S.N.*, 3/9/1818.
28 Ibid.
29 N.A., C.S.O.R.P., 1819, 132D; *D.E.P.*, 25/8/1819.
30 *S.N.*, 17/8/1824.
31 *S.N.*, 19/8/24.
32 *S.N.*, 21/8/24.
33 *Select committee report on intoxication*, letter of Graves, op. cit.
34 *D.E.M.*, 15/8/36.
35 N.A., Official Papers, 1838, 148.
36 *S.N.*, 25/8/1846; *F.J.*, 23/8/1847.
37 *S.N.*, 27/8/1841.
38 *S.N.*, 21/8/1847.
39 *D.E.M.*, 22/8/1847.
40 Monument in Donnybrook graveyard, Danny Parkinson, *Donnybrook graveyard* (Dublin 1993).
41 *F.J.*, 15/5/1855.
42 Hugh Cunningham, 'The Metropolitan fairs' in A.P. Donajgrodzki (ed.), *Social control in nineteenth century Britain* (New Jersey, 1977), p. 169.
43 *F.J.*, 15/5/1855.

44 *The Warder*, 16/6/1855.

45 *S.N.*, 1/8/1855.

46 *F.J.*, 25/8/1855.

47 *F.J.*, 27/8/1855.

48 *The Warder*, 23/8/1856

49 *S.N.*, 10/11/1859.

50 N.A., C.S.O.R.P., 1860, 17819/18577.

51 Peadar Mac Suibhne, *Paul Cullen and his contemporaries* (5 vols., Naas, 1961-77), iii, pp. 303-4.

52 *Hansard*, 21/2/1862.

53 N.A., C.S.O.R.P., 1862, 16948/17561.

54 Fergus D'Arcy, 'The decline and fall of Donnybrook fair: moral reform and social control in nineteenth century Dublin' in *Saothar* xiii, (1988), pp. 7-21.

55 *F.J.*, 27/8/1866

56 N.A., C.S.O.R.P., 1868, 16573.